D1124058

BE NATURALLY HEALED

With *The Spirit of Healing*, David Cumes offers a new paradigm
for wellness that blends Western medicine with ancient shamanic
techniques and the curative power of the wild. As a physician on
his own healing journey, Dr. Cumes has lived with the San (Bushmen) of the Kalahari and has witnessed the healing methods of
shamanic cultures from Africa to Peru. The core belief these practices share is that the process of healing is most powerfully trig-
gered when we reach a state of inner balance. That's why bodily
treatments alone are not always effective for true holistic healing—the spirit must be treated, too.

The Spirit of Healing explores a range of practices to connect
you with your higher self to empower your Inner Healer. Tap
nature's healing powers. Learn how to raise your body's healing
kundalini energy. Align your spirit with the Kabbalistic-based
Tree of Health, and explore how the concepts of soul loss and
energy fields affect the Inner Healer.

Body, mind, and spirit must work in harmony and balance for
healing to take place. *The Spirit of Healing* will help you bridge
the gap between the medical and the mystical and become an
active participant in your own healing journey.

ABOUT THE AUTHOR

David Cumes, M.D., was born in South Africa and has been a wilderness traveler most of his life. A urologic surgeon, he specialized at Stanford Medical Center, where he also taught. He currently has a private practice in Santa Barbara, California. In contrast to his classical training in a profession that relies so heavily on science and analytical reasoning, he has pursued a personal quest that evokes intuitive and introspective capabilities; he is the founder of Inward Bound, a travel company that takes healing journeys into remote wilderness areas. He is also the author of *Inner Passages, Outer Journeys* (Llewellyn 1998), which complements the experiential component of these journeys, and describes the theoretical basis for the healing and transformational power of nature. His new book, *The Spirit of Healing*, takes this idea into all walks of life.

TO WRITE TO THE AUTHOR

If you wish to contact the author or would like more information about this book, please write to the author in care of Llewellyn Worldwide and we will forward your request. Both the author and publisher appreciate hearing from you and learning of your enjoyment of this book and how it has helped you. Llewellyn Worldwide cannot guarantee that every letter written to the author can be answered, but all will be forwarded. Please write to:

David Cumes, M.D.
℅ Llewellyn Worldwide
P.O. Box 64383, Dept. K196-1
St. Paul, MN 55164–0383, U.S.A.

Please enclose a self-addressed stamped envelope for reply, or $1.00 to cover costs. If outside U.S.A., enclose international postal reply coupon.

THE
SPIRIT OF
HEALING

Venture Into the Wildeness

to Rediscover

the Healing Force

DAVID CUMES, M.D.

1999
Llewellyn Publications
St. Paul, MN 55164-0383

The Spirit of Healing © 1999 by David Cumes, M.D. All rights reserved. No part of this book may be used or reproduced in any manner whatsoever, including Internet usage, without written permission from Llewellyn Publications except in the case of brief quotations embodied in critical articles and reviews.

First Edition
First Printing, 1999

Book design by Kjersti Monson
Cover design by Lisa Novak
Cover photograph by Helene Glassman/Imagery Photography
Editing and typesetting by Karin Simoneau
Interior photographs: *The Universal Idea of Polarity Balance* by Paul Cumes; *The Astronaut,* page 50, by Mario Corvetto; *Therianthropes,* pages 53 and 55, courtesy of The Rock Art Research Center, Witwatersrand University, Johannesburg, South Africa

Library of Congress Cataloging-in-Publication Data
Cumes, David, 1944-
    The spirit of healing: venture into the wilderness to rediscover the healing force / David Cumes.—1st ed.
    p. cm.
    Includes bibliographical references and index.
    ISBN 1-56718-196-1
    1. Mental Healing. 2. Shamanism. 3. Healing. 4. Nature, Healing power of. I. Title.
RZ401.C89   1999
615.8'52—dc21
                                                  99-39979
                                                 CIP

Llewellyn Worldwide does not participate in, endorse, or have any authority or responsibility concerning private business transactions between our authors and the public.

    All mail addressed to the author is forwarded, but the publisher cannot, unless specifically instructed by the author, give out an address or phone number.

Llewellyn Publications
A Division of Llewellyn Worldwide, Ltd.
P.O. Box 64383, Dept. K196-1
St. Paul, MN 55164-0383, U.S.A.
www.llewellyn.com

 Printed in the United States of America on recycled paper

ALSO BY DAVID CUMES

Inner Passages, Outer Journeys
(Llewellyn, 1998)

© 1997 by Paul Cumes

The universal idea of polarity balance, or the core truth of equilibrating the opposites so frequently encountered in nature, is key to all healing. They are symbolically represented in this figure: sun, moon; light, dark; fire, water; masculine, feminine.

I would like to dedicate this book
to all the wonderful doctors and healers who have influenced
me and who have made me the physician I am.

To all my undergraduate teachers at Witwatersrand Medical School
whose clinical expertise was unmatched.

To Professor D. J. Duplessis and the legacy of talented surgeons
under whom he trained, who guided me during my
surgical residency in Johannesburg.

Notably, to Jerry Jersky, who fostered in me
a love for the craft of surgery and who has been
a great friend and teacher ever since.

To Thomas Stamey, Duncan Govan, and Fuad Freiha
from Stanford Medical Center, whose unselfish and big-minded
devotion to academic excellence and teaching knew no bounds.

And finally, to all the indigenous healers,
African and non-African, whose amazing resources
I am now beginning to tap.

CONTENTS

ILLUSTRATIONS

INTRODUCTION

All healing involves four factors: the healer, the patient, the place where healing occurs, and the presence of a universal Field that embraces both healer and patient.

This book is a personal journey taken in an attempt to better understand different healing mechanisms and traditions. It is concerned with the principles and the spirit of healing and was inspired by my experience with the healing properties of nature, my study of ancient wisdom, and my twenty years of surgical practice. The intention of the book is to help readers gain a greater understanding of the elements of health. With these rudiments in mind, patients and healers can become informed participants in the miracle of healing and better able to make simple but intelligent decisions for their own special healing journeys.

According to the San hunter-gatherers of the Kalahari, sickness resides in everyone, but true illness will only manifest in a few. If this is true—and I hold with the San's concept—this principle is relevant to everyone, whether healthy or ill, because ultimately health is about balance and inner harmony.

All healing involves four factors: the healer, the patient, the place where healing occurs, and the presence of a universal Field that embraces both healer and patient. The book follows these four broad headings and each chapter is labeled with the predominant theme(s) of that chapter.

THE HEALER

One catalyst for someone in a tribe to become a medicine man or woman is a primary wound or a health catastrophe. Archetypal wounded healers have healed themselves in order to heal others. This healer is contrasted with the Western doctor who has no primary wound but is wounded by the educational process and the stresses and strains of patient care. An appreciation of the psychic consequences of Western medical training may be vital to the patient's understanding of what drives their practitioner. The limitations of the physician who remains unhealed—and therefore not whole—become apparent. With the knowledge of these deficiencies, a more effective alliance can be created between the patient and the healer.

Shamanic healing balances the polarities of masculine, feminine; light, dark; sun, moon; left, right; yin, yang. Shamanism validates the idea of a core truth that permeates all ancient mystical traditions. This fundamental notion of equilibrating the opposites to attain balance is omnipresent in all beliefs and throughout the text. It is crucial to our understanding of healing. When shamans are able to achieve this balance, they realize Self, heal themselves, and become powerful healers.

Also explored in *The Spirit of Healing* are the healing methods of the Kalahari San. The San healer is able to travel out-of-body and, with the help of the ancestral spirits and the Great Spirit, divine and extract the cause of the malady. The San shaman connects intimately with the Inner Healer of the patient, not only with the laying on of hands but also with their entire body. The San healing dance may be our link with the way our ancestors first dealt with illness on the plains of Africa eons ago. Other tribal systems of healing and an understanding of the Kundalini healing energy may have originated from this primal model. The San fulfill the idea of balancing the opposites by virtue of their unique hunter-gatherer lifestyle.

THE PATIENT

Patients need to understand the feminine Kundalini energy of the cosmos, since this is basic to the comprehension of the life force and hence to the vitality of their Inner Healer. Here, two of the four categories—healer and patient—overlap. The Kundalini principle is as crucial to the healing ability of the healer as it is to that of the patient. Both the Inner Healer of the patient and the healing capacity of the healer are augmented by this force.

Models such as the chakras, the Kundalini, and the biblical Tree of Life used by yoga practitioners and Kabbalists are not just obscure esoteric concepts. They give us a psycho-spiritual framework for equilibrium and for attaining expanded states of consciousness and awareness to facilitate healing. They increase our understanding of the totality of Self in relationship to the universe, an understanding that is critical to the healing process.

According to ancient mystical tradition, the realization of Self is our primary purpose on the planet. If we deviate from our higher Self, or our soul's path, we create imbalance and poor health. Each patient must find the healer and healing technique that best connects them to Self, thereby maximally empowering their Inner Healer.

Based on all these principles, this book will outline a structure for a contemporary Tree of Health that describes some practical polarities to help patients attain a state of equanimity and wellness.

THE PLACE

Patients and healers should not ignore the fact that there are not only preferred environments for healing but also certain places where healing miracles have occurred. Some places have more profound healing energies than others. Nature is the easiest and earthiest place for many of us to achieve wellness, and pristine areas in nature are favored locations for healing. Peak experiences, joy, and ecstasy—wilderness rapture—are common in the wild and are known to facilitate healing.

This book links the lifestyle of the San in the Kalahari wilderness, the power inherent in the magical plants of the jungle and the desert regions of Peru, and the concept of a sacred healing space in the form of a symbolic Garden of Eden. These descriptions highlight the importance of place in the healing equation.

THE FIELD

Healer, patient, and place are all within an infinite Field of potential encompassed by a higher force. By achieving balance and guiding their inner energies or life forces, patients and healers are able to penetrate deeper into the Field. They may also be able to harness some of the immense healing capacity of the Field. This book will explain how messages are propagated and received through the Field so patients and healers may be able to utilize them in the healing process.

Although there are some practical recommendations that can be made about the cause and the treatment of disease, the mystery of illness and the magic of healing often remain manifestations of the conundrum of life itself. We need to be humble; if we examine anecdotes from different patients—their trials and tribulations, their remissions and relapses, and their deaths—we come to realize that there are no hard and fast rules. This book is a guide to the bewildered patient and the perplexed healer who have struggled with some of these paradoxes.

THE PHYSICIAN AS WOUNDED HEALER

There are some
patients we
cannot help.
There are
none we
cannot harm.

—Arthur
Bloomfield

What drives and motivates physicians, and what factors have affected their psyche? Many doctors are casualties not only of the training process but also of the profession. An appreciation of their wounds is essential if we are to gain the most from our allopathic or contemporary Western system of medicine and understand the limitations this method imposes on healing.

THE WOUNDED HEALER

Only much later in my career did it become clear to me that the wound of the African medicine man or any shaman was different from the wound of the allopathic physician. It is frequently a physical disability, a severe illness, or a wound that turns future shamans' focus inward, enabling them to heal themselves. This leads to an ability to go "in," in order to heal others, which is different from the allopathic Western healer's woundedness—their woundedness arises out of the rigors of the training process

1

and later is aggravated by the stresses and strains of patient care. The former causes the shaman to be empathetic and compassionate and to become directly involved with the feelings and emotions of the patient. The latter leads the modern-day physician to remain objective, dispassionate, and detached from the patient's pain and suffering. This is true even in the case of psychotherapy. If physicians were selected because they had to fulfill the criteria of the ancient wounded healer archetype, they might be better able to understand the wounds their patients have to bear. If anything, wounds acquired during the training process tend to separate physicians from the suffering of their patients.

Many physicians become wounded without realizing it, and their wounds do not occur in the ancient archetypal sense. Because they are unaware of the extent of their wounds, many doctors do not recognize they are not whole. This is in contrast to the archetypal shamanic concept of the wounded healer, where the wound creates inner growth and self-awareness, endowing the healer with a greater appreciation of the suffering of others.

It never occurred to me in my medical education that there was a certain woundedness associated with the training. My only concern was the effectiveness of the learning process, and I was prepared to endure any hardship in order to become the best doctor possible. To become a highly competent allopathic physician implied a separation from one's own inner life and deeper needs. Interests, family, and friends were placed on the back burner. While I immersed myself in medical books or wandered the hospital wards, my nonmedical friends enjoyed their families, spent time in the outdoors, or partied late into the night. Financially they were also better off, since it often took years before physicians earned decent salaries and, even then, there were sometimes heavy loans to pay off. The children in medical families often grew up with an absentee parent. In too many marriages the medical student or doctor may have been significant in the medical environment but was not a fully participating "significant other" in the home. As a result of their training process, many physicians become wounded healers.

THE EVOLUTION OF A WOUNDED PHYSICIAN

Perhaps it will help to understand the concept of the physician as wounded healer if I relate some of my own personal experiences. In a subsequent chapter this knowledge will be contrasted with that of the archetypal wounded healer.

I grew up in the suburbs of Johannesburg in an ordinary middle-class family. Throughout my younger years I had a significant amount of exposure to the outdoors because I was fortunate to have two uncles with farms in the outback. Most vacations were either spent there or camping and trekking in various parts of southern Africa. Because I had acquired an affinity for wild areas, I thought my career choice would lead me to an outdoor lifestyle such as farming or veterinary medicine. However, the implications of apartheid at that time made it unlikely that I would commit myself to a rural place where the manifestations of racism were even more rampant. For want of a clear choice of vocation, I gravitated toward medicine, and never seriously contemplated what effect this decision would have on my inner being.

Long after I had completed my medical training, I had a dream. I was in a cold, stark anatomy hall, barefoot on the cleanly mopped floor. The stench of preservatives and death pervaded the room. There were no cadavers, only body parts bathed in a type of oil and laid out on tables. There were a few students, and my dissecting partner was a tall fellow who was dissecting out one of the nerves of the forearm, but even when he demonstrated it I could not see the structures clearly. I was dressed in suit pants, a white shirt, and tie, with no shoes or socks. There was a feeling of mild revulsion as I walked on bare feet, hoping not to step in anything unpleasant, and a similar feeling of disgust when some oil from a cadaver section splattered on my shirt and I did not know how to clean it up. I would first have to go and wash my hands.

One of the lecturers entered. They were always larger than life, even in the dream, with a familiar sneer and arrogance. Every student understood that this person had complete power;

the lecturers could demean because of ignorance, and dazzle with their brilliance. We always called them "sir" and gave them total respect, knowing we did not have the knowledge to stand up to them and hoping that they would either not see us or leave us alone. Certainly, the biggest dread was that they would ask a question in front of the class that we could not answer. In my dream, this imposing lecturer began to give a prosaic rendition of the undersurface of the foot, demonstrating how this section represented a certain part of the body and that section another. His explanation was more like reflexology than anatomy, but I knew he had the right to diverge from the reality of dissection. We did not. I turned around to him in my dream and said, in a complimentary fashion, "But that's poetry, sir."

The study of anatomy had the potential to be a type of poetry, but certainly when I entered my second year of medical school I failed to appreciate this. The morbid surroundings of the anatomy hall had managed to creep into my subconscious even years later in this dream.

My second year of medical school was a difficult, dreary year of anatomical dissection. There were four students per cadaver. Teachers boasted that we were lucky to be studying in South Africa, since there was no shortage of bodies. Life was cheap. Many unclaimed souls found themselves in the anatomy halls, mostly unfortunate blacks who had come to the big city to fulfill their aspirations. They encountered death many miles away from their homes, and their dreams and spirits were lost somewhere among the high-rises of Johannesburg. Many black Africans believe that for the spirit to rest peacefully, the body needs to be buried at home. This would not be the case for these unfortunate people.

My impressions of anatomy were somber, dominated by the frustrating dissection of shriveled structures in our withered subject, the odor of formalin, and the process of tucking the body in at the end of the session with a plastic shroud to prevent it from drying out. There was also a pervasive smell, and even washing one's hands several times did not quite get rid of it.

I will never forget the first day we walked into the anatomy halls. We filed around the cadavers and sat down on the benches, waiting for the anatomy lecturer to give his introductory talk. I remember him saying two things—the first was that those of us who had studied Latin would find anatomy quite easy and those who had not, even easier. (So much for my five years of Latin at school!) The second was to deliver a set of statistics: how many of us would die as a result of cancer or heart disease, and what percentage would die due to suicide or alcohol or drug addiction, which claimed an astoundingly high death rate among physicians. This was my first inkling that there was a real possibility for psychological pain in the profession. In the subsequent clinical years, medical students were divided up into "firms," a small group of twelve individuals. Much later, two members of our firm committed suicide from drug abuse—the professor's prediction proved eerily correct.

Medicine extracts a high price from those who commit to it. This may not always be as dramatic as death and suicide, but it can be insidious in many ways. Many of us are not even sure what kind of price our inner being has had to pay for becoming the physicians that we are.

After the initial shock of being introduced to a cadaver, it did not take long before we felt at home and even befriended our mute companion. We would put our feet up on the dissection table and eat lunch or a snack. There were often light moments and jokes to release the tension. Different manifestations of insanity came to the fore, and unbelievable bets were made. One student asked how much we would pay him if he swallowed the Buchal pad of fat (a small piece of fat found during the dissection of the muscles of the face). The eye of the cadaver was dried out during embalming, so when it came to dissecting the eye we were given a fresh ox eye instead. Another student offered to swallow this as a dare. Both students were duly rewarded for swallowing these distasteful items. My second year of medicine was the most appalling I had to endure, but these temporary manifestations of lunacy helped to diffuse the pain and tension.

My third year consisted of the study of pathology, pharmacology, and physiology. Pathology was even more grueling than anatomy, but at least interesting and, therefore, more bearable. I became acquainted with the autopsy room. The mortician admonished us to "moof along, moof along" (which meant move along, move along). His grasp of the English language did not equal his ability to scalp the head, saw off the calvarium, and slit open the abdomen and chest. In this way, the mystery of death could be revealed to the pathologists and they would impart it to us.

The pathologists were more larger-than-life than the anatomists. They could think and deduce, not just memorize the intricate details of anatomy parts. They pointed to the different manifestations of disease and put it all together in a brilliant story. I found myself fascinated—maybe there was still a place for me in medicine.

Pathology was known to be the most difficult of subjects. The head of pathology was an erudite maniac who, like some of the other faculty, projected a lot of his own internal pain and woundedness onto the students. He entered the lecture hall promptly at 8 A.M. each morning and locked the door behind him. If a student was thirty seconds late it was too bad, they would just have to make up that section and borrow notes from a friend. A fellow student, Raymond, once got to the lecture hall just before the lecturer. Being the polite, terrified student he was, Raymond allowed him to go through the door first. With that, the professor promptly closed the door and locked it, leaving Raymond outside.

Stories were rampant about malicious, vindictive examiners. One external examiner from Cape Town was known to be particularly sadistic. He would draw a gallows on a piece of paper while examining his students, and with each mistake would sketch another component of the gallows. If, by the end of the oral exam, the gallows was complete with a likeness a students neck in the noose, that student knew what the outcome was. There was no question that a form of psychological warfare was waged against students in order to make them into competent doctors. It resembled military training and contributed to the developing wound.

The last three years of the training were spent on the wards with patients. This was far more enjoyable. The emphasis was on clinical teaching: how to listen to the heart, how to feel the abdomen, how to examine someone's chest or neurological system, and so on. At last, I knew I had made the right decision. The suffering had been worthwhile and I was on the right road after all. The medical training that I had in South Africa, though arduous, was a superlative and unique experience, and I am grateful for what it gave me. Africa also worked its magic on me; it was the African wilderness I turned to for healing at periodic intervals along the way of my medical training. Without the medicine of the African bush, I knew I could not have been whole. The wounding had begun, but a remedy was available. It was in Africa, in retrospect, that I first appreciated the importance of a supportive place and of nature and "wilderness rapture" in particular in the healing process.[1]

Internships were often sources of deeper wounds for the fledgling physician. They consisted of obligatory rotations through the disciplines of internal medicine and surgery. I interned in the professorial surgical unit. This appointment was given on merit but often the brightest students declined the honor due to the heroic demands required in the interests of patient care. The professor of surgery was called "God" for short. This was not entirely sarcastic, since the example he set was somewhat godlike. He asked for excellence and gave more than excellence himself.

He was an awe-inspiring clinician and a meticulous surgeon with incredible skill and judgment. When he entered a room, one felt his sheer presence. Even surgical consultants older than he stood up when he entered and called him "sir." "God" was the God of the Old Testament—impeccable, fearless, and fair, but wrathful. If his commandments were not kept, punishment was quick and sure, usually in the form of severe humiliation and, occasionally, dismissal.

Every Wednesday and Saturday there were grand ward rounds that involved a huge entourage of surgical consultants, registrars, interns, medical students, and nurses. If one's presentations were not flawless, extreme embarrassment in front of all these people was inevitable. On Wednesdays, after the grand ward rounds, the morbidity and mortality session of the week took place. Here, all the complications and deaths of the preceding week were reviewed, followed by a witch hunt for any chance of mediocrity. Perplexing referrals from other physicians came to the ward from far and wide, with the expectation that the professorial surgical unit would solve any diagnostic or therapeutic problem.

All gods are psychic and our professor was no exception. He was able to divine what had happened to a patient without knowing the full history, and could decree what would happen if the correct surgical intervention was not performed. Just as a medicine man would throw the bones to divine illness, there were times when I felt the professor was throwing his own mental bones to make an accurate diagnosis. If a subtle detail or a test had been forgotten, he knew it intuitively.

A friend of mine, Aaron, who preceded me on the ward told me of an arduous night he spent admitting a lot of critically ill patients. In those days most laboratory tests, such as blood counts and urinalyses, were unavailable after hours and interns had to perform the tests themselves. The one thing he had omitted that night was a white blood cell count on one of the patients. The professor asked for the result of that test the next morning. When Aaron replied that he did not know the answer, "God" asked him, "Why not?" Aaron said he did not have time to do it. To which "God" replied, "Did you have time to go to the bathroom last night, Smith?" Aaron affirmed he had gone once, in spite of the fact that he had been up all night with the admissions. With that, "God" countered, "If you had time to go to the bathroom, then you had time to do the white cell count." This was the level of excellence that was expected.

I spent six months in this ward and learned more about surgery and self-discipline than I could have anywhere else.

Other than asking relevant questions, the professor never said more than one sentence to me during my six-month stay. At the end of my internship he asked me what I was going to do next, and when I replied, "Surgery," he looked somewhat dubious and said, "I never realized that you were interested in the subject."

I returned to his ward as a surgical resident several years later, taking pride that I had never suffered the humiliation endured by other interns and registrars at his hands. That changed, however, one eventful Friday night when a middle-aged woman with a gangrenous left leg was admitted from an outlying hospital. She had been misdiagnosed as having a spider bite. The leg was black and had been neglected so long that there was the classical line of demarcation between live and dead tissue.

Every patient on the ward had to be seen by a consultant, no matter how obvious the pathology or the treatment. None of the patients would suffer the diagnosis of the resident trainee alone. There was a specific chain of command and a senior surgeon had to be called. I described the problem to the consultant on duty that night on the telephone. He correctly noted that there was nothing to be done and that at some elective time an amputation would be in order. He declined to come in to see the patient. Knowing the rule, I insisted that he see the patient the next morning before grand rounds. He agreed to come in the morning, but I had doubts as to his commitment. Having been trained in the United States, we viewed him as a bit of a renegade who adhered to the maxim "Question authority!"

In the flurry of the next morning's activity to get everything perfect for grand rounds, I asked the charge nurse if the consultant had seen the patient yet. She said he had not. We entered the ward and everyone crowded around as I presented the problem. The treatment seemed obvious and there appeared no need for additional questions. However, in his usual telepathic way, the professor asked pointedly, "Who was the consultant on call?" I divulged the consultant's name. I expected the next question to be, "What did he say?" and I would have responded that he had said the patient needed an amputation. However, the professor often knew what went on behind his back and suspected that Doctor X often broke the rules. His question was very specific. "Did Doctor X see the patient?" and to this I had to reply truthfully, "No."

All hell broke loose. In front of the huge cavalcade of people, the professor charged that the patient had been grossly neglected by not being seen by a consultant, and blamed me for it. He ordered me to call the vascular consultant immediately. I went to the phone and managed to get him off the golf course. We continued on our ward rounds while the specialist made his way to the hospital. It was clear that a commandment had been broken and a precedent had to be set so clearly for posterity that it could never happen again. Upon examining the patient, the vascular surgeon agreed that there was nothing else to be done and an amputation was in order on the next elective surgical list.

Nevertheless, I bore the brunt of the furor; this type of mediocrity was not acceptable and the professor had an ingenious way of making his point. He would lambaste and castigate his resident to teach him a lesson and, at the same time, indirectly convey the message to the consultant. It was a clever teaching system. By condemning a scapegoat, he could illustrate all the lessons of the day by directing the charges of incompetence at a lowly resident, even though blame often lay with the more senior person. Unfortunately, the culprit was not there that day to receive the wrath. I tried to take it lightly, since I knew I had done the right thing and no one had suffered for any lack of judgment. The next day, the professor asked me if I had told the consultant what happened, and I replied affirmatively. He asked if the consultant had been ashamed of himself, but I said nothing.

My mentor and friend, Jerry, guided me in a surgical direction and after my internship I applied to be an instructor in the anatomy department so I could study anatomy in greater depth, spend time on physiology and pathology, and pass the difficult exam required for entrance to a clinical rotation in general surgery. I overcame my aversion to the subject and entered the anatomy halls for a second time. I spent a year dissecting, studying, and teaching anatomy and at the end of the year most of us passed the grueling examination with a sigh of relief.

After that I embarked on a five-year clinical rotation to become a general surgeon. The rotation in cardiothoracic surgery epitomized the most unpleasant aspects of the education process. The chief of the unit was hated by everyone and was called "The Pig." In the operating room lounge was an effigy of a pig, with a supply of pins readily at hand. On particularly bad days, the pig would be stuck full of pins. Although the effigy was in full sight for everyone to see, the surgeon it represented never recognized his likeness in the symbol. Maybe if we had had more sympathy for the cardiac surgeon's tortured soul, it would have been more compassionate to have the pig labeled "Wounded Healer," and already stuck full of pins. On days when the surgeon was particularly malicious, instead of placing more pins, some of those already present could be withdrawn to release his inner pain.

Although we had to deal with other lamentable members of the teaching faculty, there were many lighter aspects to those years. The more serious have been highlighted to give an appreciation of what many physicians have to go through in order to become the healers they are.

Many years later I was on an excursion to Peru with psychologist/anthropologist Alberto Villoldo, who has written extensively on shamanic healing. It was to be an experiential journey of active participation in shamanic ceremonies that would be used for healing members within the group as well as local Peruvians.

The group was inclined toward holistic healing and shamanism, and I was the token allopathic physician. Most of the people in Alberto's group had nothing but contempt for allopathic medicine. I used what I thought was a clever analogy and explained to them that they had no trouble using Western technology such as airplanes, computers, and videos. They would not travel to Peru by ox cart, so why did they fail to appreciate the benefits of Western medicine? My analogy seemed to fall on deaf ears. I learned a lot during that trip about different attitudes regarding modern-day physicians and high-tech medicine.

This group was offended by the "bad energy" of Western doctors and preferred to take their chances with alternative methods. Western physicians were considered technicians, not healers. Nevertheless, on more than one occasion, some of these holistic devotees would report to me about their intractable diarrhea, which had failed to disappear with the help of their homeopathic remedies. One or two tablets of antibiotic later, they were cured of the malady, but I never heard them change their philosophy.

In spite of initially being skeptical about the ramifications of shamanism, something began to unfold slowly within me and, although my intellectual side was strongly saying "no," something was getting through to my intuitive side. To the members of the group, however, I represented the medical establishment whom they regarded as adversaries to their diverse methods of healing. This may have been my first exposure to a sentiment that is becoming more prevalent in the West—an extreme antipathy, distrust, and even dislike or hatred for the allopathic physician.

In addition, it may be that the deeper effects of physician woundedness are becoming more apparent to the worldly, modern-day, well-informed patient who may now be saying for the first time, "Physician, heal thyself before you attempt to heal me." Thus a vicious cycle is set up where the wound in the healer creates an adverse reaction from the patient, and this in turn leads to more tension and wounding in the doctor. In this way, lack of trust and disrespect on behalf of patients toward the medical profession continues to fuel the wound. With hostile patients, the litigious ethic in the United States, and insurance companies controlling patient care, many physicians are now wondering why they went through all the pain and suffering of their medical training in the first place.

In order to withstand the vicissitudes of the training, physicians have to develop and secure a strong ego. It is often the ego and its associated arrogance that gets in the way of healing. It is ego that leads physicians to believe they know best. It is ego that enjoys the patient who shuts up, follows instructions, and falls into the role of the passive victim with the disease. It is also interesting that in the wilderness trips I guide, the physicians that participate are often the hardest to get along with. Strong egos combined with a need to control can be hard to take at close quarters.

It seems that the doctors' makeup and woundedness is multi-factorial and complex. It probably begins with what compels them to go into medicine in the first place. For many there may be a hidden childhood wound that causes them to gravitate into the profession. For me, I often think that my mother's prolonged illness and final death when I was quite young led to a commitment to achieving perfect health. I felt it was less relevant if I died or not; I just did not want to be sick or an invalid. Studying medicine and keeping fit may have been my way of controlling this fear. It may be that physicians wish to understand disease so they will be able to manage or prevent their own potential to develop sickness and pain. The same may be true for psychiatrists and psychotherapists in terms of psychological illness. It is therefore ironic that early occult wounds may actually be aggravated by the arduous schooling and the demands of patient care.

Within the profession, it is well known that certain specialties, such as cardiac and neurosurgery, seem to attract the most egocentric and difficult personalities. This was one of the reasons I gravitated into urology. Most urologists seemed to be a happy, less egomaniacal lot. The bigger the childhood wound, the more the stress and strain of the specialty, and the stronger the ego, the less happy the inner being of the doctor. Their own unhappiness, gloom, and sometimes frank depression is then projected onto patients and others. The right of the patient to choose the correct therapy for their own condition is crucial in the healing process. Wounded physicians with big egos may have difficulty with patients who want to maintain control over their own disease. Just as psychotherapists are required to undergo therapy, perhaps physicians should undergo some formal process to understand their motivations for studying medicine and, if necessary, heal themselves first.

THE BENEFITS OF PHYSICAL PAIN—
A PERSONAL STORY

Ah, a wounded healer, we need more of those.

—Patient's comment to the author

Recently I had occasion to renew and refresh my understanding of wounded healer. This wound was more true to the typical archetype than prior wounds gleaned in my profession.

Following a wilderness trek to Peru several years ago, I said goodbye to the group in Cusco and started making plans for a trip to Manu Park, Peru. This is a remarkable area of pristine virgin rain forest, teeming with wildlife and looking much as it must have looked for thousands of years. Juan, my guide, informed me that we needed to hire a four-wheel drive vehicle to get us into the jungle, and from there we would go on to Manu by boat. We left Cusco and traveled along the stark, high altiplana, heading east on a horrendous road toward Pilcopata, the first substantial jungle town. After a tedious two days of travel, with one calamity following another, we finally arrived at Salvacion. The river was near the town, so we rented a boat from there to take us into Manu. After a fascinating visit to this primeval rain forest, we made our departure out of the park. It was clear that we would not be able to make it all the way back to the vehicle in one day and would have to sleep another night in the jungle outside the park. The boatman found a village on the river bank. We secured the boat at a small dock and looked around for a camping spot. There was none to be found. The banks of the river were full of reeds and marsh and looked unsuitable. There was an empty hut up on stilts, and Juan suggested that I put my tent inside. Erecting a tent within a hut sounded silly, but I had no mosquito net and the only protection from the insects was inside a tent.

I climbed the stairs into the hut and saw that the top stair, instead of being flat, sloped downward. I made a mental note of that, since I knew that climbing up in the dark might be a problem. I erected the tent within the hut, made myself comfortable, and went down into the village to have supper with Juan, the boatman, and some of the villagers. After the meal we turned in because we wanted to get an early start the next morning.

I spent a restful night and remembered dreaming, but was motivated to get up at 4 A.M. and make sure the boatman and Juan were ready to go. It had rained the preceding night, and as I left the door of the tent I noticed that the boards of the hut were particularly slippery. I took care to go down the stairs with caution. I grabbed the railing to my left with my left hand and began to negotiate the first step, which I was quite aware was abnormal. In spite of all my attention, it felt as if I was pushed by a hidden force. As I put the pressure of my left foot onto the upper stair, deciding everything was stable, something went wrong. My feet slipped out from underneath me and, because I held tight with my left hand on the railing, I somersaulted off the platform with a twist, falling six feet down onto the jungle floor below with my left hand outstretched. As I hit the ground I felt a sickening snap and realized I had broken my wrist. I groaned, not in pain, but in despair at the thought of being unable to do surgery for another two months.

I walked slowly back to the hut where Juan and the boatman were preparing breakfast, trying to think of a suitable way to get myself out of the jungle with my now grossly deformed wrist, without too much pain and suffering. It was ironic that I would be unable to treat myself. I had left my sophisticated medical kit in Cusco and had brought only a few rudimentary supplies for my own use.

We cut up my sleeping mat and found a piece of plank, which we bound securely with a bandage as a splint. I found a pill bottle to place under the palm in order to support my wrist, which looked like the typical dinner-spoon deformity of a Colle's fracture. I had only three codeine tablets, but with these and my arm resting against my body I was able to endure a reasonably comfortable boat ride.

As I sat in the boat reflecting on my fate, my dream from the night before popped into my head. I had been so intent on leaving that morning I had not remembered it when I awoke. The face of my friend Paco had appeared clearly in this dream. There had been nothing else to follow and no content to the dream.

Paco was a Spaniard who had spent a year working in Johannesburg with me as a surgical resident. He was an accomplished orthopedist who had come to South Africa to get more experience in general traumatology. We had spent many nights on call together, exchanging expertise. He would teach me orthopedics and I would help him with general surgery. The most common fracture we had to deal with was a Colle's, the very same one I had just sustained. Paco had a particularly ingenious way of reducing the break and maintaining the forearm in a cast. There was always at least one of these fractures on any given day or night we were on call, usually a child who had fallen out of a tree or off a bike. I had not seen Paco for twenty years and the last time I thought of him was nearly that long ago. My dream seemed to be warning me about a potential trauma and maybe even a Colle's fracture, but the apparition did not permeate into my waking consciousness until it was too late.

It took us six hours by boat to get to Pedro and the Toyota. We set off immediately on the road for what was to be the worst four-wheel drive ride I had ever experienced—the bumping and the bouncing caused searing pain, since the splint did not completely immobilize the fracture. The codeine had worn off and I had no medication.

We decided to stop in Pilcopata, where there was a small health clinic. After talking to the doctor in charge it was apparent that the strongest pain medicine they had in oral form was Tylenol (paracetomol). He recommended an injection of an obscure remedy that I was unfamiliar with, and pointed me in the direction of the nurse who was to give it. I had the ampoule in hand, but when I saw the injection apparatus I recoiled in dismay. It resembled something out of a Florence Nightingale scene—an old glass syringe and a needle rested in a white kidney dish, with the needle in an alcohol-soaked cotton ball. I was not going to allow anyone to inject me with this medieval device! I headed back to the Toyota, where I had a few syringes for giving antihistamines and injected myself before we took off. The effect of the medication made me severely nauseated, and the next half-hour found me vomiting out the window of the vehicle as the pain continued. Our driver drove through the night, and we arrived in Cusco at about four in the morning. It had been about twenty-four hours since I had fractured my wrist.

We headed for the state hospital emergency room, which was empty and looked more like a jail than a medical facility. A nurse in charge informed me that it would be impossible to find an orthopedic surgeon until nine o'clock that morning, when I should present myself to his clinic. I explained that I was a surgeon and my hand was extremely important to me. She was uninterested and said she would either summon the intern on call to fix it, or I could wait five hours and hope the orthopedic surgeon could fit me into his busy schedule. She refused to allow me to call him.

At that point, Juan remembered that there was a private facility, the Fernando Clinic, with an orthopedic surgeon on staff. We arrived at the clinic at five in the morning. A nurse put her head out the window and shouted to us to go away and return at eight o'clock. Again, I patiently explained the predicament. My arm had been fractured for more than twenty-four hours and I was extremely concerned, since my livelihood depended on the function of my hand. She responded immediately, called the orthopedic surgeon, and pulled me into the clinic.

A short, portly Peruvian with graying hair arrived on the scene. I was delighted to see him. He seemed to know what he was doing and took me upstairs to the fracture room. He proceeded to manipulate the fracture without any anesthetic. There was significant muscle spasm, since the fracture was now a day old. It required two strong people pulling on either end of the hand and arm with the surgeon manipulating in between to overcome the spasm and align the bone. I could feel the grating while he manipulated it, and groaned in agony. When I protested at the discomfort, he asked if I would like to be given a general anesthetic. I promptly decided to avoid the added hazard of being put to sleep. It took four attempts to get the fracture in decent position. I had never suffered such pain in all my life, and I believe that after that episode I could endure anything. Paradoxically, when it was over, I felt an extreme feeling of gratitude for the surgeon who had caused the suffering. The orthopedist placed my arm in a cast, and soon after I flew back to Santa Barbara, California.

The saga, however, had not ended. A surgeon friend of mine, noting the position of the fracture to be in good alignment, decided to place me in a softer, shorter, and more comfortable cast. He recommended that I see him again in a week. A few nights later I had a dream that the fracture ends had slipped. Instead of paying attention to my dream, I waited for my scheduled appointment. The cast was removed and an x-ray showed the bones had moved, looking very much as they had in my dream.

My friend gave me a local anesthetic block of the arm to manipulate the wrist back into place. By this time, however, nature had partially done its healing and the deformity could not be reversed. He assured me that the result was good enough, even if not perfect. "Functionally, you will be fine," he said as I gazed down dubiously at the crooked result. I recognized that my surgical skills would not suffer, but had serious misgivings about being able to perform some of the more intricate arm balances involved in my yoga practice. Over the succeeding months I gradually regained full use of the arm; the resulting poor alignment never affected my surgical expertise, but my yoga skills did suffer a little.

At first I searched for the good that I thought must come out of this experience, but failed to find it. Nevertheless, when the dust settled, there were some definite changes in my psyche, many of which I do not fully understand. In some strange way, this fracture was a rite of passage for me in which new understandings, clarity, and insights resulted on many different levels. My yoga became less goal oriented, and I was able to be in the process of the posture rather than looking at the end point of attaining it. I also became better able to separate my needs from my wants and learned to be less attached to the outcome of certain situations.

What struck me most, however, was a statement a patient made to me when he came into the office and saw me with my cast. This man was an exceptional patient who had an advanced form of prostate cancer with a very guarded prognosis. He had accepted his disease with equanimity, grace, and dignity. He knew he could not beat the malignancy, but lived happily within its framework, taking in all the lessons the disease had to teach him. The cancer had spread to his lymph glands, his liver, his lungs, and his penis. From the minute I had taken over his care, this patient became an inspiration to me. When he saw my cast he turned around and said, "Ah, a wounded healer. We need more of those." This statement was penetrating, and after that I recognized less of a duality between me and my patients. The patient and I were both wounded and healing to some extent or another and, within this new framework, I was able to be more compassionate. My model for disease was approximating more closely that of the San people of the Kalahari—namely, that sickness resides in all of us, but illness develops in a few. Any tendency I had to be an arrogant physician was lessened by the richness of this experience.

Most healers see the patient only as being ill. They cannot see that there is more to that person beyond their disease. The patient becomes merely a case, and soon is classified into a nice or demanding patient, an interesting or a boring presentation, a conventional or an unusual problem, a squeamish or tough person, an easy or difficult challenge. The patient's personality may make it difficult for the physician to see beyond this to the greater picture of that person's inner suffering. Just as the doctor cannot appreciate their own wound, they cannot see the patient's hopes, motivations, fears, or concerns. The doctor assumes an "I am healthy" aloof role and does not recognize that they may be wounded as well, or may have some degree of sickness residing within. The patient, on the other hand, realizes that to please the doctor they must become dependent and play the role of the diseased victim.

A friend of mine recently developed a limp and after three months of tolerating the pain in her hip she eventually visited an orthopedic surgeon. Before the examination, she was quick to point out her passion for wilderness and backpacking. The surgeon x-rayed her hip, diagnosed osteoarthritis, and pronounced his sentence: "Your hiking and backpacking days are over, but you can swim or ride a bike! As long as you can manage the pain that's OK, but you will probably be back here within two years for a new hip." She left the office completely devastated by the prognosis and thinking life as she knew it had come to an end. The surgeon did not "see" his patient, nor did he recognize her intense spiritual connection to wild places or the effect that his statement had on her inner being. All he saw in his limited perspective was a diseased hip, and all his frame of reference had to tell him was that sooner or later this hip would need replacement. He made no attempt to tailor his comments to the psyche of his patient.

The sufferer may fail to realize that they have their own inner healing capacity and that this power is the key to healing and the ultimate source of the cure. The good physician knows this and, in humility, is able to help the Inner Healer of the patient do the job by facilitating it, not hindering it. This is where clinical judgment plays its most important role. Good judgment comes to the fore when this dynamic is recognized. Poor judgment manifests when decisions are made based on the physician's ego and an attitude that intellect and technology are all that matter. The best medicine occurs when there is an alliance between doctor and patient rather than a situation in which the physician assumes total control. The optimum relationship is democratic rather than autocratic, one of alliance rather than reliance.

Healers who are unconscious of their own wounds or who cannot deal with them are more likely to ignore this inherent healing mechanism. The physician who recognizes the Inner Healer within is able to see both the wounded and the healthy part of the patient, just as they can see the wounded part of themselves. An alliance can be forged between the patient's Inner Healer and the outer help that the physician has to offer. This help is always given in humility, knowing there is a mysterious force at work with which we need to align. For millennia healers have paid homage to this Inner Healer. In the current era where the seduction of technology is so overwhelming, we need to do so even more. This crucial component will be discussed in later chapters.

The balanced healers of today are part shaman and part high tech physician. They realize that they do not fully understand the mysteries of healing and work within this framework. They pay attention to psychic forces and use intuition as well as intellect, compassion as well as the latest advances in the field. They recognize that each patient is different and, therefore, requires a different psychological approach to trigger their specific Inner Healer. It is just as crucial to understand which patient has the disease as it is to know which disease has the patient. If physicians themselves are not whole, the healing will inevitably be hampered.

THE DREADED MS

Physicians in the United States are fond of quoting what I call the dreaded Ms, which make their lives intolerable. These are managed care, malpractice, Medicare, Medicaid, MediCal, and for many, a mortgage and a marriage that has become dysfunctional as a result of all the stress. These Ms have further aggravated the woundedness. In the United States, physician burnout has reached epidemic proportions. Managed care, together with loss of autonomy, appear to fuel this syndrome. An inability to be sympathetic to the patient's plight is a telltale sign of physician burnout. There is a widespread incidence of personal problems, family problems, and even substance abuse among doctors because of overwork or disenchantment with their calling. It is usually the most caring and dedicated physicians that are the most disillusioned because of their idealism, high expectations, and total commitment to medicine. Physicians tend to be highly individualistic, independent, and autonomous, and often cannot express emotions and feelings or reach out for help. Many have been unable to nurture themselves or find avenues for self-expression outside of medicine because of their total dedication to healing. Having invested so much time and energy in the profession, they find it hard to come to grips with the fact that their career choice may have been incorrect. Many are in denial but an increasing number, when asked, will openly admit they would not choose medicine if they had to do it all over again.

The physicians of today—because of the forces working against them, the dreaded Ms and others—are wounded to some degree, and this wound may be hidden from their awareness. Physicians need to restore and replenish themselves for their own sake and the sake of their patients. I am reminded of this when the flight attendant instructs passengers to first put on their own oxygen mask before assisting a child or someone else. Before physicians can help someone, they must heal themselves. A drowning person cannot rescue someone else who is drowning.

Where are physicians to go to do this? Some may ski, sail, fly, play music, windsurf, read, and exercise. Very few turn to the more esoteric, inner-directed Eastern traditions, such as yoga, meditation, or tai chi. A few may embark on a course of psychotherapy, but usually for another reason such as marital strife, depression, and so on.

What is clear is that healers need a way to turn inward, since everything around them is trying its hardest to turn them outward. Some inner healing practice is needed to help connect with the intuitive and empathetic, as opposed to the purely intellectual and cognitive. Furthermore, if doctors can maintain a connection with their inner beings, they can tap into their latent shamanic capabilities and more easily heal not only themselves but also their patients. Later in the book, it will become clear that there is a certain core truth that applies in all instances of healing, wholeness, and health, and that physicians need to understand it as much as they understand medical science. If we can balance the polarities inherent in this core belief, we can easily achieve wellness.

NOTES

1. Cumes, David. *Inner Passages, Outer Journeys.* St. Paul, Minnesota: Llewellyn Publications, 1998.

OTHER ARCHETYPAL FORCES AND THE HEALER

Archetypes are crucial in understanding how we interact as humans and, therefore, are critical in the doctor-patient relationship and in the healing process.

Carl Jung, the famous psychiatrist, used the term archetype to describe a common theme that is found in all traditions and cultures. For instance, the tree represents the union or connection between heaven and earth. These essential ideas can be found in stories, fables, tales, legends, myths, symbols, and dreams, and can help us understand who we really are. They are part of our subconscious and, according to Jung, also part of what he termed the "collective unconscious." They can be thought of as being akin to the instinct of an animal—possibly something rooted in our DNA, and an essential part of our psyche and cellular memory since the beginning of time. Without an understanding of archetypes, we are less able to appreciate what moves and motivates our spirit and the spirit of our doctor, consciously and subconsciously.

The following archetypes relevant to healing will be discussed: the hero, the warrior, the persona, the Self, and the shadow.

As we will see, the hero archetype will decide how much the physician brings back to the community; the warrior will encourage a "win, never lose" attitude and contribute to the material success of the physician; the persona will determine which car the doctor drives, what clothes he wears, and what the office decor looks like; the Self archetype fashions commitment, dedication, and idealism; the shadow archetypes (and the persona) may get in the way of compassion and caring. To the detriment of their patients, most physicians do not enter the profession as a result of the wounded healer archetype, which has already been discussed.

THE HERO OR HEROINE ARCHETYPE

The archetype of the hero's or heroine's journey is a spiritual quest that fulfills all the same criteria as a rite of passage or a trial of initiation. Anthropologist Arnold Van Gennep originally described the three phases of initiation that are also common to the hero's journey.[1] These are: separation or severance, especially from the opposite sex, threshold or the process itself, and incorporation or integration back into the tribe.

After responding to an inner calling, the initiate begins the journey by separating from the constraints of ordinary life. Through synchronicity or a serendipitous event, an instrument of power is given to help the initiate on their way. This was often a sword in the days of old, but in modern times is more likely to be some form of knowledge from a guide, a friend, or a teacher. The heroine must respond to this calling or risk killing something deep within the psyche. She must also overcome the first obstacle of resistance, which may arise from her own fear or from the attempts of family, friends, or peers to dissuade her from the task at hand.

After the separation phase, the heroine enters the threshold, where she must confront her physical and psychological fears by facing the "dragon," or whatever stands in the way of the quest.

This is the second level of resistance. Once these fears have been overcome, the heroine returns to her people with the grail, or the gift of knowledge, which must now be given back to the community in the incorporation phase. As we will see, the warrior's journey has no such altruistic motive, although the warrior does complete the first two phases of the journey.

Initiation ceremonies, or rites of passage, have held much power for generations of aboriginal cultures. These ceremonies are formal processes to mark the transition from childhood to adulthood.[2] In the case of men, this rite took the form of an ordeal, both physical and psychological, that proved to the society that the boy had taken this great step. The boy separated from his mother in a psychological sense and became part of the adult male world under the tutelage of the elder males. Among many African tribes today, this rite of passage is still intact, and ritual circumcision is a significant part of it. Hunting an animal may be another part of the process. The women have similar rights of passage celebrating the beginning of menstruation and womanhood.

In some cultures, a boy must endure the psychological and physical pain of removal of his foreskin without anesthesia or a sharp scalpel. This is something few of his counterparts in the Western world would be able to endure. As the saying goes, "What doesn't kill you, makes you stronger." Herein lies the power of these ancient traditions. The initiation is formally ritualized and acknowledged by the elder males of the tribe in attendance. The youth will carry this memory all his life and retrieve it when the need for courage and fortitude arise. Armed with this past experience, he can believe in his ability to handle whatever comes his way.

Any worthy shaman has been through their own initiation, and the same can be true of the initiation, or the heroine's journey, of many would-be allopathic physicians. It is, therefore, no surprise that many physicians identify knowingly or unknowingly with the hero archetype.

Medical school, the internship, and residency for specialty training can fulfill all the preconditions of a rite of passage. In South

Africa it was done in such a way as to make it feel like a trial of initiation. We were trained to endure not only academically, but also psychologically and physically. This training began with long days and nights of studying. An effective tool for punishment against lack of knowledge was to demean and belittle the student, and teachers were masters at doing this. Once patient care became involved, the cruelest twist of all was a reminder that ignorance and lack of judgment could actually kill someone. The internship and residency were punctuated by grueling marathons of work, both day and night, always with a concern that, more important than the student coming out of it alive, the patient had to do so as well. The process was formally ritualized, as are more ancient initiations. The modern ceremony consists of a certificate of competence at the end, along with the prestigious letters—M.D.—which will decorate the name thenceforth.

There has been recent criticism of the training system in the United States; some have argued against this arduous ordeal and have said that a trainee functioning without sleep could compromise patients. I believe the doctor does function adequately, and the human body and psyche have reserve power. When called upon to do so, the doctor can cope, making the training a rite of passage in the complete sense of the phrase. If it is done in the right way, with honest and pure intent, it will lead to an excellent result. The U.S. armed forces cannot train a Marine by being soft, and the same rigorous standards must hold for the healer who deals in life or death situations. There is a certain wisdom that needs to be perpetuated. The rites must continue; they develop character, self-discipline, and staying power, albeit at the expense of wounding the physician. Any intelligent candidate can do the book work, but there is far more to it than that. Character, intellectual integrity, responsibility, resilience, and self-reliance are some of the qualities that need to be inculcated and nurtured. The wound imposed by the rigorous training can become the physician's strength, much like the remembrance of pain from the initiate's circumcision. There is a price to pay for this wound at some level within the doctor's psyche, but this is the sacrifice that must be dedicated to patient care. The cliché "no pain, no gain" does apply.

Commitments other than medicine may complete the process to a greater or lesser extent, but it seems that when life and death, pain or suffering, and fear or terror are involved, the archetypal properties of the trial are more likely achieved. The ritual is momentous and the certificate at the end is the equivalent of the grail.

The most difficult phase is incorporation, where the demands of Western materialism are such that a physician may fail to bring something back to the community and complete the final stage so all may benefit. The modern physician may have fulfilled the separation and threshold phases, but the incorporation phase introduces new dilemmas. Is fee-for-service medicine truly bringing something back? A doctor in private practice is running a business and, unless otherwise funded, a doctor providing service without a fee will go broke and his family might suffer. The Kalahari San shamans in southern Africa now charge for services rendered, whereas previously, healing was given for free. It would be interesting to see how this has changed the interaction among these small bands of closely knit people. A wealthy shaman who disturbs the egalitarian nature of the group may generate less powerful healing potential due to jealousy and resentment. From the perspective of healing, material wealth may bolster ego and acquisitiveness, and for the purest healing to occur, the ego needs to step aside. In this way, only the good of the patient is considered and there can be no other hidden agenda. The San Bushmen believe that this power is given by the spirits and the Great Spirit as well. If it is given freely, should it not be passed on freely?

Salaried academicians and other practitioners appear more likely to fit into the phase of incorporation. They receive their pay regardless, and can afford more attention to performing the art for its own sake. Nevertheless, in the United States, the pressure to "publish or perish" disturbs the balance. It is not enough to take care of patients and teach residents. Medical academicians must prove their worth to the board of the university or the powers in charge by bringing enough prestige or money into the institution for research. Only in this way do most get the security of tenure. I spent five years at Stanford Medical Center, and it was startling to see the institution lose some of its finest clinicians and surgeons. Although their clinical results were outstanding, their dedication and focus on patient care resulted in a lack of research, which failed to bring big grants into the institution. They left because of job insecurity or because their contracts were not renewed.

The emphasis on research was transferred to students, interns, and residents, who quickly realized that if they wanted to get anywhere in the academic world, research grants and lab work were crucial to their success. Just as private practice may be a business, academic medicine can become a similar enterprise. Academic medicine is very often a hotbed of politics that further detract from the completion of the incorporation phase.

For the physician healer who has no interest in running a business, doing research, or writing, there does not seem to be a way to associate with the full-power of the hero or heroine archetype. The society suffers because the doctor is not able to realize the incorporation phase of the heroine. This final phase seems lost in the modern world and, at best, is a pale example of the knight's return with the grail. It becomes difficult to bestow one's healing talents with pure altruism within the constraints of Western custom.

The hero archetype is fulfilled during medical training since most students, interns, or residents are not preoccupied with financial remuneration and are wholly dedicated to the task of patient care. As the resident on call at night in the more peripheral black hospitals around Johannesburg, we were frequently on our own with an intern and, although consultants were available, we were reluctant to call them out. If we did, it often took forty-five minutes or longer for them to get to the hospital, and sometimes this was too long.

On one occasion, I was called urgently to the emergency room to treat a young male who had been stabbed in the chest. I was a junior resident and had not seen, let alone performed, cardiac surgery. One, however, did not have to be a genius to recognize the telltale signs of a stabbed heart. Bleeding had occurred into the pericardial sac (the sac that encases the heart), and was causing a tamponade. This meant that the tension caused by bleeding into this sac prevented blood from entering and leaving the heart. Blood was trapped around the heart; I could not hear the heart sounds. In addition, the neck veins were beginning to distend to enormous proportions and, since blood could not enter the heart and be pumped away, the patient was in severe shock.

As we transported the patient directly to the operating room, I told the nurse to contact the surgeon on call and tell him to come immediately. I opened the chest with the help of an intern and exposed a spurting left ventricle through the pericardial sac. Just then, the consultant entered the room. He helped me stitch up the ventricle and, although the chest incision might not have been the most classical one to use for the problem, it served the purpose. The patient left the hospital a few days later, none the worse for my efforts. Experiences like these enabled us to tap into the hero archetype, and the exhilaration of such events more than made up for the cost of the wounds sustained by the all-consuming training process. In fact, the two in many ways were inseparable.

THE WARRIOR ARCHETYPE

It is important to distinguish between the hero and the warrior archetype. The modern-day physician has no difficulty fulfilling the criteria of the warrior. Simplistically speaking, there is a battle or challenge to confront, and one has the option of winning or losing. As good Americans, we are conditioned to believe that there is nothing good about losing.

As a parent, I was always amused at the beginning of the soccer season when the coach would talk to the kids. "We're all here to have fun and not necessarily to win," he would say. "My objective is for everyone to play the game and have a good time." As the season progressed, and the parents and the coach got more serious about being on the winning team, this lofty ideal rapidly eroded. When the team needed a goal to win, the child whose chance it was to play remained on the side lines. In this way, a youth learns the rules of Western conditioning—the only thing worth bringing back is success. Let the others contend with the feelings of failure. The warrior works in the world and brings back the prize for the employer, himself, and his family. Rarely does it go beyond that.

The American dream is all about becoming a masterful warrior. This ethic results in material success, but also causes suffering. The hero, on the other hand, gains nothing materially, but is given the gift of inner peace and satisfaction. There are no winners or losers.

Rabindranath Tagore wrote:

I slept and dreamt that life was joy,
I awoke and saw that life was service,
I acted and behold, service was joy.

The hero brings something back to the people, while the warrior has no such philanthropic motive. In the case of the hero, material loss can mean spiritual gain.

Those who identify with the hero archetype have difficulty carrying out the incorporation phase, since Western tradition does not understand or reward true selfless behavior. Our culture may appreciate and admire it, but we are suspicious of our heroes and look for hidden motives. Although successful warriors are numerous, a true hero is a rare phenomenon today, and the medic is unlikely to gain respect without the outer signs of success that our convention admires.

It seems that although many physicians complete a trial of initiation during training and embark on a hero's journey, they arrive only to find the final phase of incorporation impossible to fulfill. Disappointment leads to more suffering, which deepens the wound. At best, most embody and enact the archetype of the warrior. There is a war to be fought and they fight the good fight, sometimes prevailing and other times not. When they win, they find it only fleetingly gratifying, if at all. When they lose, for instance, because of the dreaded Ms working against them, they are demeaned and depressed.

It is not surprising that some physicians decide to donate their services and work within inner city ghettoes, or travel to third world countries where they can administer their talent and fulfill the incorporation phase. Others connect with the hero archetype in activities outside the profession.

THE PERSONA AND THE SELF ARCHETYPES

The persona, or mask, is an archetype that we all hold dear. This is the face we wish to present to the world so we will be acknowledged in a favorable way. Our persona reflects the house we live in, the car we drive, the clothes we wear, the partner or spouse we choose. Our persona also changes depending on the circumstances, the people we meet, and the image we wish to project; it is different at home and at work. Since it is so unstable, the Hindus and Yogis called it Maya, or illusion. They knew that the true or higher Self lay beyond the persona and the ego, or the small self. The persona is different from the real Self, described by Jung as the totality of the whole psyche, the inventor, organizer, or source of our dreams and inner aspirations. The persona is representative of ego, and the Self symbolizes the soul, higher Self, or that divine essence made in the image of God, our Christ, or Buddha nature. How far our soul develops depends on how much the ego is prepared to listen and subordinate to the messages of Self. If we succeed in making ego and persona subservient to Self, we become individuated, self-actualized, or self-realized.

THE SHADOW ARCHETYPE

The shadow archetype represents unattractive aspects of the psyche that have been repressed; these aspects frequently manifest as undesirable parts of the ego. All components of the ego are essential for our development; they help highlight those aspects of soul or Self that need to come into being. It is only by identifying our shadow side that we can see which direction the light is coming from. Again, this confirms the validity of the core belief of opposites that will be discussed later in the book—there can be no light without dark, no yin without yang.

We are unable to recognize a negative aspect of another person unless it is part of our own shadow as well. Like recognizes like. We "project" aspects of our shadow onto others and, in this way, our ego is able to feel good about itself. Judgment and blame of others are powerful manifestations of the shadow. When physicians judge their patients in an unfavorable way, more often than not the shadow side of the psyche is operating. Lack of inner balance and burnout aggravate this occurrence.

It may be that ego, persona, and the warrior archetypes are driving the physician to achieve the prestige and financial gain that accompany the profession, but their motives may still be in line with the authenticity of Self. The problem arises when the doctor becomes the persona and forgets the dream behind the dreamer. In this way, the shadow can predominate by forming a powerful alliance with the persona and ego. All forces of darkness are in collusion and Self is put aside. The healer identifies more with the external trappings and status symbols of modern living than the pain and suffering of his patients. Arrogance arises, dictating that "I know what is best for you, what is right and what is wrong, even if it does not fit within the comfort zone of your inner being."

The story of my surgical professor in chapter 1 illustrates two things. First, his primary motivation was always for superlative patient care; second, although he had a strong shadow side, his quest for surgical perfection kept him aligned with his sense of

Self. It was for this reason that, in spite of his harsh methods, he was admired and respected, even fondly, by those around him. His integrity and authenticity with Self were rarely at issue.

In contrast, I am reminded of a friend who was admitted to the intensive care unit in status asthmaticus, an advanced state of asthma that could not be controlled with the usual treatment. She had to have a tube placed in her windpipe to assist breathing with a respirator and was put on massive doses of cortisone. She was recovering well, but one of the enzyme studies (which go up when someone has a heart attack) was minimally elevated. The physician, feeling the need to impart all available information to his patient, told her that not only did she have bad asthma and terrible lungs, but she had suffered a heart attack and heart damage as well. (The diagnosis later proved to be incorrect.) She was given these bad tidings while still being ventilated by the machine, and could not talk because of the tube. There was immediate deterioration in all her measurable parameters. Her heart rate, respiration rate, and blood pressure rose significantly, and the degree of spasm in her lungs increased. The family who had listened to this tactless physician were appalled and requested another physician take over her care.

The second specialist was no better. When he reviewed his colleague's records, he ignored the home history, which noted that it was only when she had asthmatic attacks that her lung function was compromised. He confirmed the erroneous diagnosis of severe irreversible emphysema and gave a guarded prognosis when, in fact, she had led a completely normal life with very few restrictions. The second physician aggravated the patient's condition further by saying she would be a "lung cripple," in a wheelchair and on continuous oxygen for the rest of her limited life. Imagine his shock when she walked into his office two weeks later, back to her old self and with favorable reports from the respiratory therapist confirming the family's history.

Everyone knows that physicians can be wrong, but when doctors, without thinking, proclaim negative prognostic information to a patient who is under duress, it can only have a harmful effect—an example of ego and shadow prevailing over compassion and common sense. Fortunately, in this case the patient was able to rise above the doctor's dire predictions, but many cannot. Even if the prognostications are likely to be true, as healers we should stress the good and favorable unless the patient demands to know the worst. Even then, words should be chosen carefully. When Hippocrates said, "Do no harm," he was not only referring to physical harm; psychological harm may be just as damaging.

The hardships of managed care, fear of malpractice, and other negative aspects of modern-day medicine aggravate the situation by belittling the value of the physician and the hero's journey. The disconnection between the ideal of medicine (as motivated by the Self of the healer) and the reality of the system (often driven by the shadow of big business) becomes complete. Physicians untrained in esoteric philosophy or Jungian psychology do not understand the ramifications of this divorce and feel cut off from their soul. This causes further deterioration in the healing relationship between doctor and patient.

The patient, on the other hand, develops a lack of trust, and their own shadow arises to assign judgment and blame, instituting litigation for anything less than a perfect result. Both physician and patient need to ask the question: "Do ego and acquisitiveness have an ulterior motive behind my behavior?" If so, the shadow is more than likely working behind the scenes. Arrogance, self-righteousness, pompousness, conceit, disdain, and presumptuousness can all be manifestations of the shadow of the physician. The desire for financial gain in a system that supports litigious action may be driven by the shadow of the patient.

Archetypal behavior is part of the human condition and helps us fashion the way we are and the way we behave. Archetypes are crucial in understanding how we interact as humans and, therefore, are critical in the doctor-patient relationship and in the healing process. Understanding these archetypes may allow physicians to recognize and deal with their deficiencies and their motivations. Patients who understand these forces will be able to help their doctors maximize their skill and talent.

NOTES

1. Madhi, Louise Carus, Steven Foster and Meredith Little. *Betwixt and Between: Patterns of Masculine and Feminine Initiation*. La Salle, Illinois: Open Court, 1988.

2. Van Gennup, Arnold. *The Rites Of Passage*. Chicago: The University of Chicago Press, 1996.

A LOOK AT THE SHAMAN

Shamans are healers, seers and visionaries who have mastered death. They are in communication with the world of gods and spirits ... Above all, however, shamans are technicians of the sacred and masters of ecstasy.

—Joan Halifax[1]

To understand how healing first began, it is vital to appreciate the concept of the shamanic healer. Here lie the roots of healing that still hold good to this day.

The shaman represents a contradictory polarity to healing when compared to our modern allopathic paradigm. A psychological or physical wound may cause a member of a tribe to become a shaman. The average medical student, however, has no overt wound when they begin the training, but is wounded in the process. The shaman embraces mystique rather than methodology, the compassionate and the empathetic rather than the objective and the impersonal, the intuitive rather than the rational. Shamanic techniques are a side to healing that have largely been ignored by Western medicine. The marriage of science and shamanism creates equilibrium and fulfills the requirement of balancing the opposites for more complete

39

healing. The recently created term, "medical intuitive," is a polite and acceptable term for a Westerner with shamanic powers. The best physicians should be cognizant of the latest technology and be part shaman at the same time. However, if they find their shamanic abilities lacking, they should at least be open to the fact that these talents can be extremely useful.

Modern day neurophysiology has its own core notion of balance and tells us that the brain can be simplistically divided into two halves, left and right. The left is the masculine, cognitive, intellectual side of the cerebral cortex. It also involves such qualities as will, endurance, goal orientation, drive, competition, and ambition. By analogy, it would be connected to the third chakra, or the sephira of Yesod, on the Tree of Life (see chapter 6). This is the side of the brain that is intimately connected with ego and makes us feel good about our achievements. Our Western education has developed this side of the brain to the detriment of its opposite.

The right side of the brain, on the other hand, is the feminine, receptive, creative, intuitive part of the cerebral cortex and is involved with the more subtle qualities of love, empathy, and compassion. In this way, it connects us with the higher Self. Shamans and mystics have been expert in accessing this side of the brain, which is the gateway to spirit. Vulnerability and getting in touch with feelings are crucial in experiencing these higher energies, and ego is the deterrent. Naturally, we need both left and right brain, both masculine and feminine. When we balance the two, we fulfill the universal truth of balance and attain whole brain function. Unfortunately, the emphasis on left brain function permeates all aspects of our life and, unless we make a conscious effort to connect with the right, we will not achieve whole brain mastery nor will we attain more complete healing.

Shamanic activities facilitate right brain activity and are by their nature inwardly directed. They include ceremony, ritual, drumming, chanting, singing, dancing, fasting, solitude, meditation, and the use of plant hallucinogens. Many shamans are creatively and artistically inclined. Shamans have known for eons that these sacred techniques help them and their patients balance the body's energy system, and the ultimate expression of this equilibrium is contact with the soul or higher Self.

The word shamanism conjures up something obscure and esoteric, but most physicians growing up in South Africa were well aware of the many traditional healers that practiced in the community. More often than not, local black people would visit these healers before finding their way to allopathic physicians. Often these medicine people were derogatively called "witch doctors," and the whites did not have much respect for them. True witch doctors did exist, and these sorcerers dealt with the dark side of occult power.

Rae Graham is an ordained white nyanga in South Africa. Her classification of traditional healers in South Africa is complex.[2] There are *nyangas, mungomas, sangomas, valois,* and *wizards.* Most whites in South Africa are familiar with the more common terms: nyanga and sangoma. Nyangas look at the general health of the patient in relationship to the family and the community. They divine the problem or illness by "throwing the bones," then prescribe remedies, often in the form of medicinal plants. They may see the source of these natural cures in their dreams. Their approach is holistic, and they are not only diviners and herbalists, but diagnosticians and psychologists as well.

Sangomas do not work with bones, but go into a trance-like state and speak in strange voices. They are said to communicate directly with the ancestral spirits to perform both individual and community diagnosis and treatment. (Today's equivalent in the West would be a trance channel.) In times past, each chief would have his own sangoma, who was greatly feared. The sangoma would smell out undesirables and use them as sacrifices to appease the spirits. Sangomas were known to be able to point to an unfortunate victim and turn him into a zombie. They work with powerful forces and are more like a specialist diviner, whereas nyangas can be likened to a form of general practitioner.[3]

The shaman uses altered or ecstatic states of consciousness and out-of-body spirit flight to gain knowledge about the diagnosis and treatment of the disease or problem at hand. This unique ability may be hereditarily transmitted, arise spontaneously out of a dream or vision (bestowed by the spirit world), or occur because of election by the tribe. Sometimes the calling arises out of a deformity, disability, illness, or even a form of psychosis. In other words, a "wound" may create the shaman, thus generating the true "wounded healer" archetype. Some shamans are self-chosen, but they do not usually wield as much power.

To most whites in South Africa, however, sorcerers, witch doctors, nyangas, and sangomas were regarded as one and the same and their primitive power was felt to rest on the superstitious beliefs of their followers. When practicing medicine, we often witnessed some of the complications of their trade: profoundly sick people who had resisted the hospital until the last moment. Many times, doctors regarded the traditional healers as being responsible for this, but they never looked carefully into the matter.

Some of us realized that African healing was similar to Western healing, in that there were good healers and bad, just as there were skillful physicians and incompetent ones. Unfortunately, it was usually the charlatans that we came into contact within the hospital ward. The real traditional healers were known to have significant abilities. They could throw their bones and tell amazing things; they could divine the future, localize the source of illnesses, find lost people, and establish direct contact with the supernatural. Like sincere shamans everywhere, they helped their people and guided daily events with the use of their knowledge of what was to come. What was clear, however, was that they did have real power, but it was easier for whites to discount it out of hand than to try and grapple with something that made no sense to the Western mind. In earlier times, the apartheid policy made exploration of the subject more difficult.

My first contact with a nyanga was when I was about ten years old. I was very fond of Samuel, our family's cook, who came from

Sibasa, in the north of the country, an area I later learned was renowned for its healers. He was kind and gentle and artistic, often a talent of shamans. He would sculpt wonderfully detailed animal figures for me which I could never replicate. He was in his late fifties, somewhat overweight, not particularly handsome, mostly bald, and quite paunchy.

I noticed that on his afternoons off, he had strings of visitors. What interested me most was that many of these visitors were young, attractive women. I began to believe that Samuel was a ladies' man and had some inherent attraction that I could not comprehend. Later on, when his entourage of attractive females increased, I became suspicious. Being a curious child, I sneaked into his room one day when he was out.

The room was immaculate, with his neatly arranged furniture polished to a sheen. Samuel had even rigged a clever contraption to his light switch, a device with a cord and a series of levers and pulleys so he did not have to get out of bed on cold winter nights to turn off the light; he could simply pull the cord that hung next to his pillow.

The bed was raised on bricks. This was to prevent the Tokolosh, an evil spirit, from attacking while asleep at night. The Tokolosh, or Thikoloshe, is a small hairy man about the height of an adult's knee, with only one buttock and a long penis that he carries over his shoulder. Fortunately, he is short and cannot climb, hence the effectiveness of bricks to raise the bed.[4]

The bedspread hung down, almost touching the floor. I lifted it, and underneath were the tools of his trade: bones for throwing. Flat bones and knuckle bones—the divining bones of the nyanga. Even at my young age, I realized that Samuel was an important person, and that his frequent female visitors were not his lovers, but his patients. I seem to remember there were some other unsavory items under the bed, such as dried-out parts of a dead animal. At that point, the Tokolosh loomed large in my mind and I made a hasty exit. I regret I never talked to Samuel about his profession, but he probably would not have shared much with me anyway. At that time, the white man's arrogant attitude was all-pervasive, making blacks reluctant to share information.

Now when I visit South Africa I go with a different attitude. Whenever I have the opportunity, I visit with indigenous healers and talk to them about their healing.

David Malalazi is an old friend who had worked for the family in Johannesburg when he was a teenager. He is a Matabele from Zimbabwe; strong, handsome, proud, and intelligent. During a shamanic ceremony in the Amazon jungle, I had a vision of David and me roaming around Matabeleland in Zimbabwe together. We were exploring places in the bush, including some old ruins—the scene was particularly vivid and stuck in my memory.

On a trip to South Africa several years ago, I decided to take along my son Paul, who was then seventeen, and my youngest daughter, Romi, who was twelve. Social interaction with David was always uncomfortable when we lived in South Africa because of the laws imposed by the apartheid regime, but David came and lived with us for a few months on several occasions when we lived in California. On one of these occasions, Paul had a friend over to play, who asked him innocently, "Who is that man? Is he your father?" "No," Paul replied, "but I think he is my grandfather." When I heard this interaction between the two of them, I realized I had made a good decision in immigrating to America. The purity of the conversation was such that there was not even a hint of the racial discernment he would have developed if he had grown up with apartheid.

Shortly before I left on my visit to Zimbabwe, I had separated from my wife Carol. We were going in diverse directions at the time and felt the need to live apart and see what transpired. I wanted to visit Zimbabwe, and my vision in the Amazon came back to me. David was working as a freelance gardener in Johannesburg and went back once a year to visit his family in Plumtree, Zimbabwe. Plumtree was close to the places I wanted to show Paul and Romi, Hwange Game Reserve and the Victoria Falls, so I wrote to David and asked him to meet me in Bulawayo. We would travel together for a week and spend time in Hwange and Victoria Falls, then David would go back to his family in Plumtree.

When we arrived at Victoria Falls, David decided that he wanted to walk around the town, so I asked him to find me a traditional healer. With my marital separation, I had reached a junction in my life and felt in need of additional insight. Being a local, if anyone could find me somebody reputable, David would be the one.

When I met up with David later that afternoon, he told me that he had found a "strong" nyanga. In his typical fashion, he had thought nothing of spending his whole day satisfying my request and had researched the situation in great detail. Eventually, David chose this healer after sitting outside his hut. The criterion for his decision was that this nyanga was a happy man, unlike the other he had visited, who seemed to have a dark side and did not smile. The one David chose was popular, and during the course of the day many people, both black and white, had gone to see him. David showed me the way, and I entered the nyanga's small hut while David politely sat outside.

I sat on the ground as the nyanga threw the bones. San and Bantu healers in southern Africa make use of bones for divining. There are bones for male and female, strong and weak, black and white, fast and slow, and other universal polarities that are important for attaining the essential balance required for divination.

I still looked, dressed, and talked like a South African, so I was particularly surprised when he told me that I came from a faraway place. He also told me that he saw trouble in my home—big trouble. He said the situation with my wife was serious, but he did not see divorce in the bones. At that time, I was inclined to disagree, since Carol and I had not been getting on well and I had actually thought the separation was final. (In the short-term he proved to be more accurate than I, since after I returned to California from South Africa, there was a reconciliation which lasted several years.)

He proceeded to tell me that I had many friends in South Africa, that I was a doctor and healer, and that in time I would begin to use traditional African methods of healing, such as he used. (In subsequent readings, two other nyangas told me the same thing.) He intuited that my dreams were chaotic, which was true—though sometimes prophetic, they were jumbled, and I had little control over them. He told me he would give me some special *muti*, or medicine, to organize the dreams better, but I declined when he suggested a price of 140 Zimbabwean dollars. I gratefully paid the consultation fee and gave him a handsome tip to boot. I had gotten more than my money's worth from the old man.

As I exited the hut, two young Afrikaners approached, talking Afrikaans to each other. They intended to go in together, and asked me how it had been. "Excellent," I replied in Afrikaans, but suggested they go in separately for a more personalized reading. Things were changing in South Africa. This was the surest sign of respect from an Afrikaner—the ex-architect of apartheid—a request for healing or advice from a Matabele medicine man.

A year earlier, I had spent some time with Credo Mutwa at his healing center northwest of Johannesburg. Credo is a renowned Zulu sangomo who has written extensively. His prophecies are known to be unusually accurate. It was Credo who gave me the best description of an out-of-body trance state that I have ever heard, and I regret not having had the opportunity to record it.

He told me many things about myself that he could not have possibly known. The best trance channels, or mediums, speak to one's inner being, and when heard, the words have impact at a deep level. They have the ability to put people in touch with their own inner truth or higher Self with carefully selected phrases. Mr. Mutwa castigated me for leaving South Africa. He spoke to the depths of my soul and said, "Africa is dying, the people are dying, the traditions are dying, the animals are dying. What are you doing in America? You should be working here. This is where you are needed!" He also gave me some insights into my personality and character, so profound that only friends and family close to me would have understood.

Paul, who was a teenager at that time, was also in the circle. He told me later that as the sangoma had begun his divining, he had thought to himself, "What a load of nonsense." At that instant, Mr. Mutwa looked at him with his piercing eyes and told him telepathically that he had heard what he thought. Paul was alarmed and embarrassed, and rapidly changed his opinion about the old man.

Another master shaman I was privileged to meet was Eduardo Calderon[5] who came from the northern desert area of Trujillo in Peru. Eduardo would perform all-night ceremonies for healing and, although skeptical at first, with time I came to recognize that he was a man of vision with real healing power. His model for illness and disease was not unlike that of the South African Bantu. They believe that disease or bad luck is often imposed from the outside by someone wishing them harm. Sometimes these evildoers have enlisted the help of a witch doctor or a sorcerer (*brujo* in Spanish). In order to cure the patient, the hex, spell, or evil spirit needed to be exorcised. This is different from the Kalahari San Bushmen, who believe that illness comes from the spirit world. The San model is less divisive within the group, since there is no fear or suspicion that malevolent occurrences may be coming from one's neighbor.

Eduardo would go into a trance-like state with the use of a hallucinogenic San Pedro cactus preparation. The mescaline and other psychoactive additives in the brew would open his "third eye" and his ability to diagnose the source of the disease, which then could be extirpated in a ceremonial manner. This was done with the help of assistants, ceremony, chants, the use of rattles and, especially, the use of his mesa (a ceremonial table).

There was no question that Eduardo seemed to identify people in the group who were in need of healing, and ignored those who were healthy psychologically and physically. The reason he gave for the malady usually seemed to ring true for the sufferer, and the benefits, at least in the short-term, were obvious. Others have confirmed the long-term benefits of this type of healing. There seemed little doubt that Eduardo was able to read peoples' auras and their subconscious minds. He insisted that nothing happened by accident and made reference to "power" animals that had symbolic meaning; these power animals will be discussed later in this chapter.

On a second trip to Peru, Eduardo was joined by a jungle shaman, Augustine Rivas, who later conducted the Ayahuasca experience recounted in chapter 6. Both Eduardo and Augustine were well-balanced, humorous, robust characters with great presence and personality. Besides being able to cure organic disease, these shamans could bolster self-image and restore confidence to overcome specific social and psychological circumstances that were troubling their patients. The shamans were even more powerful among Peruvians in their own cultural context.

Eduardo worked by balancing good and evil. He did this from the base of his mesa. On the mesa, he would lay out power objects in a set pattern. The good artifacts were on the right, or the light side, the evil were on the left, or the dark side, and the middle field was the mediating center between them. Many of the northern Peruvian shamans use the same principle of balancing the two forces. Eduardo would talk about this dynamic in terms of magnetism, or electrical force.

Eduardo explained further that the field to the right was the field of justice, and to the left was the field of evil. The field of justice combated the unhealthy influences. The field of evil contained the negative forces, and here the shaman localized the cause of the sickness, which could occur as a result of sorcery or a natural malady. Depending on which it was, a different power object on the left side of the mesa vibrated, and this vibration could be identified only when the shaman was in an altered state of consciousness. With the "third eye" (sixth chakra—see chapter 6) opened by the San Pedro cactus potion, he made a diagnosis and prescribed the treatment. The mediating center in the middle of the mesa balanced the opposing fields and created the equilibrium necessary for healing.

The balancing of opposites validates other traditions that mandate that we work to equilibrate various polarities to achieve balance and wellness. The divining bones of the Bantu, the intertwining serpents of the caduceus around the central staff, the sun and moon *nadis* (channels of energy that emanate from the chakras) of the yoga chakra system around the sushumna channel, and the male and female branches of the Tree of Life (chapter 6) emphasize this universal truth. Near Paracas, in the southern desert of Peru, a huge figure called the Trident or Candelabra is etched in the sand. This archetypal cactus-like figure resembles the Tree of Life of the Kabbalah. It has three limbs: the outer two demonstrate the polarities of left and right, and the middle, a path up the central limb to the top, represents supreme balance.[6] The Trident was also a site of initiation and a place of power for Don Eduardo and other desert shamans. Eduardo explained the meaning of the Trident in much the same way as he did the mesa. The healer needed to stay balanced in the center and move the energy upward in order to heal.

Eduardo added Datura to the San Pedro and also used tobacco juice taken directly through the nostrils. The tobacco was thought to activate the olfactory nerves and then the limbic system to evoke memories. The San Pedro cactus and the other psychoactive ingredients are another way of moving Kundalini energy up the spine and opening up the seven main energy centers, or chakras. When the third eye or sixth chakra opens, clairvoyance results, creating the profound healing ability of the shaman.

Eduardo took us to the enigmatic Nazca lines in the southeast desert, where many huge animal figures are etched in the sand, as well as geometric shapes, trapezoids, straight lines, and spirals, some of them as large as one-quarter of a mile in length. They are thought to have been there at least 2,000 years, but have been discovered recently because they can be seen properly only from the air. Figures that can be seen include a spider, a monkey, a fox, a killer whale, and many birds, including a frigate bird, condor, cormorant, and hummingbird (which is the most graphic). A bizarre figure on the side of a hill that looks part human has been fondly termed, "The Astronaut."

The Astronaut

Nazca Lines, Peru. An example of a therianthrope encountered in the third phase of trance.

© 1999 by Mario Corvetto

There has been much speculation[7] about the purpose of these lines and the way in which they were formed. There is probably no single answer to their origin, and geometric shapes sometimes superimposed on the animal shapes may have postdated them by hundreds of years.

The desert shamans today regard these animals as power animals, each representing an aspect of power and wisdom. The power animal is the same as a totem animal; the shaman takes any special quality or characteristic of that animal with the hope that this "power" might help them along their path in life; for example, the hummingbird may be symbolic of endurance, and the spider, of patience.

The origin of these fantastic figures in the desert sands of Peru is still open to debate. Many scientists feel they represent astronomical and agricultural calendars that indicate the solstices, equinoxes, and seasons, and that they informed the ancient Peruvians when to plant and when to harvest. Others have suggested they were made by extraterrestrials.[8]

It might be that earlier shamans, being masters of ecstatic flight and out-of-body travel, had visions of these totem animals during their trance-like states. It also seems likely that shamans who had access to this form of power would not find it technically difficult to devise a way to etch these figures into the sand. A shaman in a trance-like state who had a vision of an animal or saw geometrical shapes and spirals might have wanted to record these for the gods and posterity. If they were able to travel out-of-body, we do not need to invoke the possibility of extraterrestrials as the architects of these lines and figures. It may have been a shaman's vision, some simple mathematics, and a lot of community help that created this spectacle.

There is an analogy between this theory and that of David Lewis-Williams[9,10,11] to explain the bizarre forms of rock art in southern Africa created by the San. According to Lewis-Williams, director of the Rock Art Research Unit at the University of Witwatersrand in Johannesburg, San shamans in South Africa probably depicted the experience of out-of-body travel and trance-like states on the rocks and caves of the subcontinent. For instance, the San artist, to represent the experience of being underwater during a trance, painted fish and eels. The desert shaman of Peru would possibly see a whale. Naturally, the shaman in trance is incapable of producing any rock art, so the renditions they made must have been done after the fact. It was felt that San shamans could "turn" themselves into any animal, including birds and lions.

A Peruvian shaman in trance may have had a vision of a hummingbird or another desert animal, and later felt the need to record this experience. According to scientists,[12] it is possible to devise simple technology with which to make the figure without necessarily being able to see it from the ground.

Many of the paintings in southern Africa depict images of animals that represented magical qualities. Eland, the largest antelope in Africa, were a symbol of potency and believed by the San to be the most mystical of all animals. Eland are a common image in San rock art. The Inuit shamans did not see eland, but polar bears; Peruvian shamans saw monkeys, hummingbirds, frigate birds, spiders, whales, and even human-like figures with faces like owls (also seen on ancient pottery), mistaken by many today for extra-terrestrials.

Lewis-Williams[13,14,15] describes geometrical designs such as zigzags, grids (lattice or honeycombs), chevrons, spirals, sets of lines, meandering lines, dots, and similar geometrical forms. These are called entoptic phenomena, and are known to occur in the first stage of trance. Since we all have the same central nervous system, the neurophysiology of trance, as studied by those having taken hallucinogens, is reproducible. Everyone experiences entoptic visions early on; these may occur with the eyes either open or shut. They occur within the optic system, anywhere between the eyeball and the visual cortex, and are related to the release of chemicals called phosphenes. After the trance, these images were likely painted onto different rock surfaces. In the case of Peruvian shamans, they may have been etched in the desert sands in the form of giant geometrical figures.

The second phase of trance is an attempt by the mind's eye to make sense of these entoptic figures. The symbol may blend into a more complex pattern called a construal. The form the construal takes depends on the person's own culture, personal experience, and local environment. In San art, there are beautiful examples of lattice or grid entoptics blending into an engraving or painting of a giraffe, which has its own unique lattice pattern. Some rock engravings in South Africa often take the form of mandalas similar to those depicted by Yogis.

Icons appear in the final stage of trance, and the trancer becomes part of the experience. In the deepest form of trance, the animals seen are believed to be real. This certainly is true for the descriptions given by Amazon jungle shamans under the influence of the "vision vine," Ayahuasca. These shamans were believed to be able to turn themselves into jaguars in the trance state, just as San shamans could change into lions. Westerners have difficulty with the concept that a shaman could "become" an animal. This may happen in a mystical rather than a physical sense, as the healer fuses with the power animal in the hallucination while in trance.

A combination of human and animal figure seen in rock art is called a *therianthrope*. The human form becomes fused with the animal and has, for instance, hooves instead of feet. These figures are all over the rock faces of southern Africa, and possibly represent shamans in trance becoming the animal itself. There are similar examples of rock art all over the planet that have been rendered by aboriginal peoples through the millennia. "The Astronaut" in Nazca may in fact be an example of a therianthrope. These representations are a testament to the shaman's ability to enter an altered state of consciousness to divine and heal.

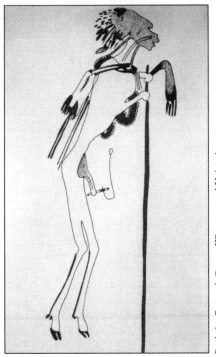

Therianthrope

Part animal, part human, this therianthrope demonstrates the type of visions seen in the third phase of trance.

(From *Images of Power: Understanding Bushman Rock Art*, David Lewis-Williams and Thomas Dowson.)

Rock Art Research Center, Witwatersrand University

All of this speculation probably would inflame scientists working on the Nazca lines today. Nevertheless, we may need to look outside of science, which attributes astronomical events to the reason for the figures. Author Evan Hadingham, after expounding eloquently on all the scientific theories in his book, *Lines to the Mountain Gods*,[16] also suggests that the out-of-body experience and the trance state may be key to explaining the Nazca phenomenon. Paul Devereux, in his book *Shamanism and the Mystery Lines*,[17] has the same idea and believes the straight lines may have represented lines of magical flight to assist the shaman in out-of-body travel, much in the way flight routes do for aircraft.

Rock art, rather than just being of historical and aesthetic interest, may be the key to understanding how some of these altered states of awareness were experienced and then artistically reproduced. The research on these trance states overlaps descriptions of the Hindu Kundalini phenomenon and includes descriptions of bodily elongation,[18] or a change in body image, dissolution of the ego, a change in the appreciation of time, and a sensation of the spirit leaving the body. This is seen in rock art as a line coming out of the top of the head. Often, the trance state is described as a sensation of being underwater or of entering a hole or tunnel in the earth.

As we will see later, plant psychedelics are not only a way to enhance the clairvoyant and facilitate healing, but are also a way of transcending ego and realizing the higher Self. For true healing to occur, patients must come into harmony with what is true for their Self. Furthermore, shamans who have realized Self in sacred ceremonies with plants, and who themselves are more whole, are better able to assist in the patient's own inner healing. Many Western physicians become disconnected with Self because of the rigors of their profession, and are thus incapable of "seeing" the souls of their patients.

Therianthrope

The line traveling out of the top of his head indicates that as the soul leaves the body in the trance state to travel to the world of spirits, there is also a change in perception of the body's configuration.

(From *Images of Power: Understanding Bushman Rock Art,* David Lewis-Williams and Thomas Dowson.)

Rock Art Research Center, Witwatersrand University

Shamanic techniques are tools that can help us attain health and wellness. The wound that occurs to physicians as a result of the medical training process is frequently a deterrent to their ability to heal themselves or their patients at a deeper level. Some of the best Western physicians have shamanic abilities and often put them to good use without realizing it. However, Western medicine has difficulty validating these nonobjective methods that are not easily measured. The portal to this alternative healing is the right brain and, for this, we need to open the heart. We need more heart in our modern system and a little less intellect.

NOTES

1. Halifax, Joah, Ph.D. *Shamanic Voices*. New York: E.P. Dutton, 1979.

2. Graham, Rae. *Tales of the African Life*. Capetown: Struck Books, 1992.

3. Ibid.

4. Hammond-Tooke, David. *Rituals and Medicines*. Capetown, South Africa: Creda Press, 1989.

5. Calderon, Eduardo, Richard Cowan, Douglas Sharon and F. Kaye Sharon. *Eduardo el Curandero: The Words of a Peruvian Healer*. Richmond, Louisiana: North Atlantic Books, 1987.

6. Cumes, David. *Inner Passages, Outer Journeys*. St. Paul, Minnesota: Llewellyn Publications, 1998.

7. Hadingham, Evan. *Lines to the Mountain Gods*. New York: Random House, 1987.

8. Ibid.

9. Lewis-Williams, J. D. and Thomas Dowson. "The Signs of All Times, Entoptic Phenomena in Upper Paleolithic Art," *Current Anthropology*, vol. 29, no. 2, April 1988.

10. Dowson, Thomas A. *Rock Engravings of Southern Africa*. Johannesburg: Witwatersrand University Press, 1992.

11. Lewis-Williams, J. D. and Thomas Dowson. *Images of Power: Understanding Bushmen Rock Art*. Johannesburg: Southern Book Publishers, 1989.

12. Cumes, *Inner Passages, Outer Journeys*.

13. Lewis-Williams, J. D., "The Signs of All Times."

14. Dowson, *Rock Engravings*.

15. Lewis-Williams, J. D., "The Signs of All Times."

16. Hadingham, *Lines to the Mountain Gods*.

17. Devereux, Paul. *Shamanism and The Mystery Lines*. St. Paul, Minnesota: Llewellyn Publications, 1993.

18. Cumes, *Inner Passages, Outer Journeys*.

THE SACRED SEARCH FOR THE SELF

Drugs allow us to taste the beyond but do not make us masters of the transcendental.

—Swami Muktananda

Today's shaman is the living embodiment of ancient archetypal healing, uniting the patient, the healer, the place, and the presence of a mysterious force, Divine intelligence, or "field" of energy. Shamanic healing links all four essentials of healing: healer, patient, field, and place. The shaman's ability cannot be separated from the environment in which they work and the remedies nature provides in that particular ecosystem. Many shamans use psychoactive plants to access their diagnostic and therapeutic talents and to facilitate their patient's Inner Healer. Shamans all acknowledge a higher force and seek to align with this power to maximize healing.

Shamans must undergo their own transformational journey and quest for the sacred Self before becoming healers. As a neophyte on the path, it struck me that participating in shamanic rituals and healing ceremonies could be a powerful way not only to connect with Self, but also to improve my healing skills. Psychedelics can induce a Kundalini experience by moving energy up the chakra hierarchy, by dissolving the impediment of ego, and by opening the heart "block" (see chapter 6). These rapturous states can be difficult for intellectual, left-brained skeptics to attain. By annihilating ego, hallucinogens can been used to obtain a glimpse at a different reality and short-cut the long, arduous road to the higher Self. For the more rigidly conditioned among us, the use of psychoactive plants can precipitate a healing journey or search for Self. The paradox is that those of us who need a "big gun" to open up to the mysterious are by our nature very grounded and, therefore, unlikely to avail ourselves of this potential catalyst. On the other hand, less grounded individuals may be easily enticed by psychedelics, and they are precisely the ones who may be harmed by hallucinogenic destabilization of the ego. When we return from the journey to our mundane existence, a well-established ego can be an invaluable companion. Eastern philosophies, Kabbalah, and transpersonal psychology have confirmed that, in order to reach the true or higher Self, we have to transcend ego. A strong ego, however, is a vital commodity, and we need to develop and nurture it before we are prepared to subordinate it on our quest for Self discovery.

Doing our healing or spiritual work with psychedelics seems to be cheating—a little like scaling a mountain by helicopter rather than on one's own two feet. The appreciation of a climb on foot to the peak is well earned, and the vistas are more true and undistorted. Nevertheless, the helicopter ride gives us an idea of what the view may be like and whether a slower, methodical ascent later is worth the trouble.

The coca leaf has been used in the Andes for thousands of years for sacred reasons, and its use has rarely been associated with negative effects. Its complex alkaloids can help adaptation to "soroche," or high altitude sickness, and keep workers going all day without food or water, as it takes away the appetite and promotes energy. It was only when Westerners separated one of its alkaloids, cocaine, that a problem arose. The coca leaf remains revered in the Andes, and no Quechua inhabitant who uses it for ritual and work would ever admit to anything other than its positive influence. The same can be said for other plants used by the local peoples in healing ceremonies in the Andes, the Amazon jungle, and elsewhere.

Plant psychedelics are hallucinatory, but not addictive. Side effects occur, but toxicity is mitigated by the fact that no single component is extracted or concentrated (as in the case of cocaine). Harmful alkaloids and chemicals present often prevent overdose by causing nausea, vomiting, and diarrhea before too much is taken.

One psychoactive plant in particular, Ayahuasca (*Banisteriopsis caapi* or "Yage"), is most interesting. This is the so-called "vision vine" or "vine of the dead" of the South American rain forest. A hallucinatory mixture is made from the pulp of the vine and other additives to potentiate the effect, which occurs as a result of complex biochemistry. The Western world is only now coming to appreciate this complexity.[1]

Ayahuascero shamans say they are able to communicate with the spirits of other plants after they have ingested Ayahuasca, the mother of all plants. By talking to the plant spirits, they are able to find natural cures and remedies from the rain forest for their patients. They claim that medicinal formulas come to them out of this psychedelic experience. Certainly, drugs like curare are too sophisticated to have been fabricated purely by chance or even empirical experimentation.

In my sojourns to the Amazon, I have been involved in a few of these ceremonies and found them most illuminating, since I am one of those who requires a "big gun" to break free of past conditioning and ego. Having grown up in South Africa where the '60s passed us by, imbibing mind-altering substances was something new to me. Certainly, the draconian drug laws at the time and my profession excluded their use entirely. Dagga, or marijuana, was readily available, but I never availed myself of it. It was, therefore, with some skepticism and a negative bias that I approached the idea of a sacred ceremony using hallucinogenic plants. My intensely conservative background convinced me that at best I would see strange things and, at worst, could go mad. I reassured myself that this was not just a "trip," as the spiritual and healing intent were predominant, and the ritualistic ceremony was orchestrated in a sacred manner by the shaman. Furthermore, I knew that the potential side effects of the plant were sufficiently uncomfortable, and one would not readily undertake such an experience unless it helped to achieve personal growth or healing.

In the course of my travels in Peru I had two experiences with Ayahuasca, the first of which was near Pucalpa in the Amazon. I had arranged to meet a shaman, Don Augustine, who was living there at the time. We arrived at the sweltering airport and were met by a sweating Connor Nixon, who at that time ran the beautiful Lodge of Las Brisas. In later years, the lodge was taken over by cocaine traffickers and Nixon was evicted from his place. Don Augustine also had to leave the area, which became particularly unsavory. It was ironic that in this area of the world there were two contrasting mind-altering substances—cocaine, with its devastating effects on human societies, and Ayahuasca, which had profound potential for healing. Cocaine was a recent Western invention; Ayahuasca carried an ancient tradition of metamorphosis.

The next day, a small group of us, including two other Westerners and a friend, Jose Luis, took off to Don Augustine's power spot in the jungle. Following a one-hour drive along the main highway, we hiked for three hours into the rain forest enduring oppressive heat. Richard, one of the local residents who assisted Augustine, led the way with his pack balanced on his back and a head strap taking up the strain of its weight. We were also accompanied by five Peruvian women who had come for healing. One woman had taken Ayahuasca before and claimed it changed her life.

Don Augustine's power place was a jungle paradise, with a river running through it and bananas and papayas everywhere. There were rudimentary platforms and grass shelters in which to spend the night. We had swum en route to cool off, but we bathed again in this river and scrubbed ourselves down with mud, part of the cleansing ceremony that was to precede the Ayahuasca the next night. We ate fried yucca and dried fish, which were excellent. That night before going to bed we were assaulted by mosquitoes. The mosquito net I had brought was not of much use. The insects came up from under the shelter and flew through the cracks in the floorboards for the attack. Rain poured down the whole night.

It was still raining when Don Augustine began preparing the Ayahuasca the next morning. The vision vine was cut into small pieces and then pounded into a fibrous pulp, which cooked at a slow boil for the entire day. Different additives were used to complement the formula, including datura, coca leaves, herbs, and sugar cane. Water was added periodically. Everything was done meticulously, with Augustine supervising and Cesar carrying out his orders.

A great discussion took place around the fire as the rain came down onto the shelter. Augustine told us that the higher the intent of the participants, the more effective the vine; therefore, a meaningful discussion around the boiling brew facilitated the experience. Ayahuasca would tell the past, present, and future, and would help with the questions asked of it. We were warned that we would probably all vomit, but we were to go beyond physical discomfort to learn from the experience. The more frequently one took the hallucinogen the better, since the knowledge it could reveal was infinite. Even children, whose basic survival instincts were intact, were encouraged to start at an early age. If it took one to a place one did not like, Augustine said to go with it. Only in this way could one relinquish undesirable aspects of one's past and, as such, it was a potent form of psychotherapy.

I became involved with the preparation of the substance and found that thinking positive thoughts allayed some of the fears I had about the ceremony to come. Due to the torrential rains, small snake-like subterranean rivers had opened up underground, one of which broke through at the base of the Ayahuasca fire and devoured it. This required that we relight the fire and move the pot, resulting in an hour's delay in its preparation. I was unsure whether this was a good or a bad omen.

Jose Luis and I were given the task of cooling the brew, which we did with large ladles, much as you would cool soup. With each movement of my hand, I would raise up the dark liquid and allow it to pour back into the pot, insinuating my sincere intent into the mixture as I did so and hoping it would treat me well. The Ayahuasca began to take the form of a personage with whom I was developing a relationship. At that time in my life I was at one of my many crossroads, and the taking of the substance seemed opportune. Maybe it could help me in defining my direction in the world outside my profession.

Again that evening we bathed and scrubbed with mud. The day with the rain, the brew, and the conversation had been magical, and the river had risen several feet. Shortly before the ceremony, the rain stopped. Augustine set up a table close to a huge old tree, which rose well above the jungle canopy. There was a white table-cloth on the mesa with numerous candles burning on it. The women in the group were set off to one side and the men to the other, except for Cindy and Paul, the two other Westerners, who were a couple. We were to drink a full cup of Ayahuasca in one go and not spill a drop. The taste was not unpleasant and was even a bit sweet from the added sugar cane.

We sat and waited for the effect as Augustine sang, danced, and chanted sacred *Icaros* (Ayahuasca chants). After forty-five minutes, it was clear to him that the brew was not strong enough, and he gave us all a second cupful from a previously prepared bottle he had brought from Pucalpa. This tasted vile, and soon after many of the group began to vomit profusely. Some of them had significant diarrhea as well.

My experiences were gentle and subtle. First, a feeling of euphoria and heightened awareness came over me. The chanting of the music seemed to penetrate into all my body cells, and I realized that an important part of the ceremony was Augustine's energy and his ability to chant these amazing rhythms into the night. The

Icaros sounded completely different under the influence of the Ayahuasca. They seemed to fulfill all the components of primordial sound, not unlike the chants the Bushmen use in the Kalahari to get into a trance-like state. Augustine played a Jew's harp, and the sounds seemed to vibrate into my soul. As we sat, he passed around a magnificently carved pipe with sacred tobacco, which we smoked and then he smoked, blowing smoke all over us in a manner of healing.

I could feel the Ayahuasca working its way down the length of my intestines like a palpable bolus. As it worked its way down toward my rectum, it seemed to carry with it all my past impurities and unfortunate conditioning.

We danced around the tree in the Amazon that night, and I remember that I had severe difficulty standing and walking. I saw none of the visions I had heard and read about, but I did experience visual patterns when I closed my eyes (entoptic phenomena).[2] Sometimes these visions were like stars, wavy lines, dots, and even mandalas, and an occasional dragon or snake floated by. Early on, there was a roaring or buzzing in my ears. Years earlier, I had visited some San in southeast Botswana and when I asked them about their mythology, they drew pictures of bees. Due to the language barrier, I could never fathom the meaning of this until after the Ayahuasca experience, when I realized that the noises in my head were like the buzzing of bees. This type of sound is very much part of the Kundalini phenomenon.

My awareness seemed more like a flow of past events drifting across my consciousness, but the events felt as real as if they were occurring at the time. I was in a vivid dream of my past life's experience. Small details and scenes bubbled up into my mind's eye; scenes I had never thought significant that had been buried in my subconscious. I now realized they were important factors binding me to past conditioning, and they needed to be released for healing.

I let them go as they floated by. These nemeses of my past were not at all unpleasant, and I could watch them with detached appreciation in that moment. I could not have done that when these traumatic events had happened. These episodes included moments of despair when, as a child, I was an inpatient in a miserable hospital in Johannesburg. The panorama extended several years later to my mother's critical illness when she was bedridden for many months, and I feared she might die. Some of the trials and tribulations of my early school life, the bullies and the sadistic teachers I had encountered, also appeared. I was the observer and these visions the observed, and both seemed intimately connected. There was absolutely no pain associated with the process of observation. All three components, observer, observed, and process of observation, had melded into a single experience and a sensation of oneness. I had a sense of unity rather than separation and, with this, the feeling of rapture rather than anguish.

As this bolus was working its way down my gut, it became symbolic of these past events. At the end of the catharsis, the sensation reached my rectum. I felt ready to evacuate the past. I went behind a tree and pulled down my shorts, but all that was forthcoming were blasts of warm air—my past traumatic life experience had translated into one long burst of air! I could not help but feel amused, and certainly I was removed from the pain of it all. Nevertheless, in spite of the irony, a healing had occurred.

There were a few other thoughts, rather than visions, that appeared, one of a friend in an aircraft which I was concerned might crash. This worried me as a harbinger of bad things, since I knew of Ayahuasca's ability to forecast events. Now, some years later, nothing has come of this vision, signifying that the occurrences are not always clairvoyant and therefore cannot be relied on absolutely. Ayahuasca also has been called telepathin because of its ability to impart telepathic knowledge, which is then used by shamans to intuit illness and heal with hands-on techniques.[3]

As the final effects of the substance started to wear off, I wanted to remain next to the primal tree on my own. Everyone except Cesar looked ready for bed and good dreams. Augustine left me with his carved staff to use for protection; he left one for Cesar as well. We watched the small group wend their way up through the forest to the platforms. Cesar sat quietly by my side, both of us in a state of reverie. We listened to the jungle sounds in the night, as an eerie mist descended upon us. Cesar walked off on his own with a flashlight for a while, leaving me to my thoughts. When he returned, we both ambled back to the platforms, and on the way found Paul tending the fire, seemingly mesmerized by it.

I slept well that night and awoke before anyone else. The huge tree near the mesa was hollow and large enough to walk into. When everyone awoke, we ceremonially went one by one into the tree and squeezed out of a small crack on the other side. Augustine told us as we squeezed through that we were now born again; I felt I had experienced a rebirthing. There was a distinct feeling of renewal, clarity, calm, and inner peace, as well as a sense of release from some of the demons of my past.

I bid my goodbyes to the group, who were going to stay another few days at the spot with Augustine. Richard took me out of the jungle and it was just as well, since all the rivers had risen and previous landmarks were obscured. I was still shaky when crossing over some of the makeshift bridges, and appreciated Richard relieving me of my camera. In some places, we waded chest-deep in water, and eventually we reached the small river where we had swam on our way in. The water had flooded its banks and could not be crossed. We were fortunate to find a native with a dugout, who ferried us over.

The meaning of the moment was not lost to me. I crossed over the body of water, aware that symbolically I had also ferried over my own unconscious. Ayahuasca had helped me access part of my psyche that I doubt any other form of psychotherapy could have done with such powerful impact.

I experienced Ayahuasca on another occasion, not as powerful as the first. The reason for this, I think, was two-fold. Subsequent shamans did not have Augustine's energy or musical talent. He had augmented the Ayahuasca with his Icaros, singing unceasingly into the night. There seemed to be a tremendous synergy between song and substance, and as soon as the song waned, I could feel the intensity of the experience fall away. Subsequent shamans had lacked the energy to chant throughout the entire ceremony. Also, my initial experience had been in pristine jungle, whereas the later episode occurred inside a jungle lodge, which lacked as intimate a connection with nature.

My next experience occurred near Iquitos, where I appreciated new lessons and was able to learn further from past mistakes. In the second experience with Ayahuasca, I felt myself standing outside of myself, peering in at my deficiencies, as if I was observing someone else's faults objectively. This seemed to be part of an ego-less state, or perhaps an out-of-body experience, and was extremely enlightening and helpful.

The heaviness and seriousness of my early life became apparent. One of the shamans picked up on this at the same time I was experiencing it. He said he saw a heavy crown on my head, one that was far too heavy to hold. I took life too seriously. The responsibilities in my profession weighed me down. "Anyone would have a difficult time wearing a crown that heavy," he said. I recall vividly at the time having a profound sensation of nausea and a sense of a heavy weight on top of my head forcing me down toward the ground. I felt as if I wanted to die.

During the ceremony, there were moments when my sense of Self disappeared into nothingness and there was only a blackness associated with empty awareness. I can describe this only as being akin to a near-death experience, and after Ayahuasca I no longer fear dying. Today, my normal flight or fight reaction is intact and I respond appropriately to fearful situations, but the thought of lying down to die does not bother me anymore.

I recall an experience in which I felt I was spewing up my innards and came to, gasping and retching. When I checked my body for signs of vomit, there were none. I was told that this was probably a type of birthing experience. Shamans have interpreted this type of panting as a feeling of being under water. Whatever the description—death, drowning, or rebirthing, it is clear that one crosses a threshold and never feels the same afterward.[4]

There were occasional visions of snakes. The snake may represent a construal where the entoptic of a line takes on the more complex form of a serpent.[5]

There were also some paradoxical effects, including an intense feeling that I did not need to do this again, that it was not part of my path or of my distinctly substance-free background. During the ceremony, one of the other shamans saw a vision of a Moses-like figure, or a spirit from the time of Moses. Associated with it was a vision of the caduceus and a menorah. He deduced from this in his trance-like state that there was a Jewish physician in the group, and that this spirit figure was his guide. Both the caduceus and menorah are very dear symbols to me.

In his book *The Cosmic Serpent*,[6] Jeremy Narby describes the prevalence of giant reptiles, zigzag snakes, intertwined serpents, and ladder-like images that appear universally in the Ayahuasca experience. Interestingly, the Ayahuasca vine itself can grow as a liana, similar to an intertwined double helix. Narby has linked the hallucinogenic serpent to the DNA helix, and extrapolated from this that Ayahuascero shamans have for eons had an appreciation of this basic structure of life through their visions.

The Caduceus

As we will see in chapter 6, the archetypal symbol of the inter-twined serpents of the caduceus is also represented in the Hindu system of chakras, in the spiraling helical nature of the sun and moon energy channels along the spinal column.[7] The Kundalini serpent energy is activated by psychedelics and may be represented in these Ayahuasca images when a single snake is involved. The idea that DNA is represented as a pair of intertwined snakes seen in these visions is entirely possible. This archetypal image is concordant with the idea of a universal truth or core belief that states that healing energy will move up the body depending on the balance of two polarities: masculine and feminine, light and dark, yin and yang, sun and moon. Moreover, this energy moves in a spiral or zigzag fashion, and the course it takes is also helical in nature. These shamans may have been having visions of this pathway as long as the Hindus and Yogis have had the appreciation of energy spiraling up the spine along twin energy channels. The Yogis also believe, "as is the microcosm so is the macrocosm"—conceivably, as is the DNA so is the universe.

I had read reports of people having visions of certain power animals such as anacondas, jaguars, condors, and eagles, and knew that in the third phase of trance, experienced shamans could fuse with or become these animals.[8] I had no experience of such therianthropes.[9] I did, however, "see" my own power animal: an elephant that crossed a dirt road and then turned to look at me in my dream-like state or vision. It was a large bull elephant in a typical African bush scene. Amazon, Ayahuasca, jungle, shamans and all, my power animal lived in Africa rather than in Peru. In studies of trance-like states, the visions in the first phase are reported to be universally the same. However, in the second and third phases they relate strongly to cultural background and local environment.[10] My African roots had a far greater effect on my experience than did the local fauna.

It also seemed that my body was a vibrational entity, and my perception changed according to the level of vibration. During the ceremony, there were spontaneous bursts of energy, both along the spinal axis, where one would expect to find the chakras or "energy

wheels," and peripherally in the extremities. Those occurring cen-
trally were sometimes very strong and appeared to be rising up my
spine. I was reminded of the descriptions of the Kundalini, as well
as the zigzag renditions of this energy in San rock art.

There were times I found myself asking, "Where am I, where is
my Self, my true Self, my higher Self?" I was met with a sense of
emptiness. In that moment, I was unclear whether there was in fact
no me! Later, I wondered whether this was part of a state that the
Buddhists talk about of reaching a state of "emptiness," where
there is extinction of all thoughts or notions and there is no sense
of Self or ego. Certainly, there were times when the Kung San
description said it best: "My thoughts were nothing in my head!"
(See chapter 6.)

After each encounter with Ayahuasca, I felt a sense of peace
rather than turmoil, bodily vigor rather than exhaustion, clarity
rather than confusion. There were none of the bad side effects
one would associate with a typical drug experience. In many ways,
I had the same feeling I had after being away in the wilderness for
a week or more—a sense of harmony and oneness, and a feeling
of completion.

I was told by one of the shamans that it took him six months
before he had visions or developed the expertise to control them
and use the Ayahuasca for healing and intuiting illness. The
mechanism of this ability to diagnose disease is the opening of the
"third eye," or sixth chakra, as Kundalini energy rises up the
spine. A similar phenomenon occurs not only during the healing
or trance dance of the San, but with the imbibing of the San
Pedro cactus preparation by the desert shamans in Peru. Shamans
from diverse cultures use different plant hallucinogens for sacred
healing and ceremony.

There is clearly more to be learned if one commits oneself to
these teachings. Such a study is best undertaken in shamanic tradition in an altruistic manner and with the goal of becoming a healer, helper, and a visionary for one's people. I believe Ayahuasca is
not for export, as it fits into the cultural context and energy of the

jungle more than anywhere else. Just as it is not logical to take the trance dance of the San out of the environment of the Kalahari, Ayahuasca belongs in the rain forest and in the cultural context of its people—not in North America, where it has created interest recently. In the popularized context of "Self-realization" and gaining one's "own" power, it could lose meaning and become just another hallucinogen. The emphasis then might be on self-absorption rather than on ministering to others.

Over the years, I have met people who explore the world of hallucinogens for self-improvement but do not possess the desire or expertise of the shaman to heal others. It seems to me that, as many physicians are often spared from the infectious diseases they treat, the shaman is spared the side effects of the plant when used selflessly for healing. When I worked in the hospitals in and around Johannesburg, we were exposed to all sorts of infectious third world diseases. I intuitively felt safe that I would never contract them. Most Westerners who use hallucinogens on a continuous basis in a nonceremonial, nonphilanthropic, and nonsacred way appear to suffer the consequences physically and mentally.

Moreover, for the uninitiated, a distorted ego can prove a formidable adversary and mimic the egoless state. What appears profound, in reality can be a deception. In this state, except in the case of a shaman with years of experience steeped in cultural tradition, one walks a fine line between distortion and truth.

Or, as Gampopa said, "A mere glimpse of reality may be mistaken for complete realization."

Ayahuasca requires perfection and learning.

One of the shamans, in a short speech before a ceremony, said, "As you sow, so shall you reap." What you put in, you get out. You cannot be what you are not, and even with the help of Ayahuasca the basic work still must be done. One must develop self-mastery as well as a strong ego before trying to dissolve into the egoless state.

It was clear that experiences with Ayahuasca differed remarkably, and mine bore little resemblance to any I had previously or subsequently read or heard about. There were no "group" visions or communications occurring telepathically among the participants,[11] although the shamans seemed to pick up on thought patterns. It did appear, however, that one got what one needed rather than what one expected or wanted. One required time to integrate the experience and much of what happened occurred at a subconscious level. There were shifts in behavior afterward that could be attributed to this experience.

From my experience, I developed a sense of clarity that wilderness was my gateway to harmony, healing, and the transcendent, and this was one way in which I wished to express myself in the world. Ayahuasca had linked me even more indelibly to nature and had opened a new door for future expression. In one of the more vivid visions I experienced, I was on a small mountaintop, or *kopje,* as it is called in South Africa. The acacia bushveld sprawled away in front of me and below me. There was a pool of water on the edge of the kopje and a small house behind it. The unusual thing about the house was that it was incomplete; the roof was not finished and stacks of tiles were piled up in clumps on the roof infrastructure. It seemed that however my expression of Self would occur, there was a lot of homework to do first.

NOTES

1. Mckenna, Terence. *Food of the Gods.* New York: Bantam Books, 1992.

2. Lewis-Williams, J. D. and Thomas Dowson. "The Signs of All Times, Entoptic Phenomena in Upper Paleolithic Art," *Current Anthropology*, vol. 29, no. 2, April 1988.

3. Lamb, Bruce. *Wizard of the Upper Amazon.* Boston: Houghton Mifflin Company, 1974.

4. Wolf, Fred Alan. *The Eagles Quest.* New York: Summit Books, 1991.

5. Lewis-Williams, "The Signs of All Times."

6. Narby, Jeremy. *The Cosmic Serpent.* Jeremy P. Tarcher, Putnam, New York: 1998.

7. Cumes, David. *Inner Passages, Outer Journeys.* St. Paul, Minnesota: Llewellyn Publications, 1998.

8. Lamb, *Wizard of the Upper Amazon.*

9. Lewis-Williams, "The Signs of All Times."

10. Ibid.

11. Lamb, *Wizard of the Upper Amazon.*

RETURN TO EDEN— THE HEALING POWER OF PLACE

What wilderness does is present us with a blueprint, as it were, of what creation was about in the beginning, when all the plants and trees and animals were magnetic, fresh from the hands of whatever created them.

—Laurens Van Der Post

Most of us feel more healthy and whole when surrounded by nature. The San hunter-gatherers of the Kalahari and other hunter-gatherers who depend on the gifts that wilderness provides may very well be the key to understanding health and wholeness. These so-called "primitive" people are (or were) fortunate in being able to live as close to the purity of this sacred space as is possible today. When we depend on nature for survival, our senses expand and we develop an entirely unique way of relating to the environment. The true hunter-gatherer lives beyond the five senses and has access to a psycho-spiritual space that we can only imagine. Pristine wilderness is the nearest thing we have today to the Garden of Eden experience, and this might also be a model for the most healthy environment. The Garden of Eden is an original blueprint or archtype for sacred space, and is highly relevant to our inner and outer health.

73

We might think that one thing Adam and Eve had before their undoing was perfect health. They lived in paradise, were favored by God, had a stress-free existence, a loving soul mate, and an excellent unsaturated fat-free diet (they were vegetarians) with all the necessary vitamins, minerals, antioxidants, and phytochemicals to sustain them. They must have taken long walks and had plenty of exercise and were presumably at one with the rhythms of nature. This life style, at least according to New Age thought, is superlatively healthy.

However, in spite of the fact that the last surviving hunter-gatherers live in harmony with each other, the earth mother, and the cosmos, they are still prone to disease and ill health. The San acknowledge that we all have sickness (imbalance) lurking within and that only in some does this turn into illness. We are no more knowledgeable than they are in understanding the basic cause of illness. They may blame disease on the ancestral spirits while we incriminate the immune system, but we are all guessing when it comes to understanding why some fall ill while others do not. How does one explain the paradox of the person who smokes, eats and drinks what he wants, does no exercise and may even be lonely and miserable, yet lives to be one hundred, whereas another, obsessed with keeping the body perfect, drops dead at fifty with a heart attack or is stricken with cancer? Modern medicine may point to genetics and New Age devotees to the power of an unhappy mind, but the question still remains.

An untarnished natural environment can promote optimal health. Nature provides multiple qualities and polarities that we cannot gain in an urban setting. Nature indeed appears to be a favored and special environment for health and wholeness. In fact, the effect of nature is so powerful for some, that the return to urban life can result in a sense of loss or a re-entry depression.[1,2] Sunsets, smells, scents, and sounds such as the wind in the trees, or so called "soft fascinations," result in restoration of that part of the brain exhausted by our hectic day-to-day existence. These images have this effect by inducing a relaxation response or a meditative state.

Nature is a potent source of awe, wonder, and at-oneness. "Wilderness rapture"[3] can be much like the "peak" experience described by Maslow. These are fleeting moments when we transcend ego and achieve a glimpse of the Samadhi-like state of the Yogi, or the Nirvana of the Buddhist. The elation possible in nature confirms the importance of place in the healing equation.

This particular chapter discusses the power of place as one of the four variables of healing. At the same time, it introduces the reader to the San healing dance. Certain places in the world are renowned for their healing properties, or "energy," and there are numerous locations around the globe where the local people will say exceptional cures have occurred. One of the most famous of these is Lourdes, where the Vatican has set up a panel of doctors to objectively decide whether certain patients have been miraculously cured or not. Numerous miracles have been proclaimed at Lourdes by the Vatican's Medical Commission. The mechanism for these cures could be attributed to the belief of the patient (the placebo response), Divine intervention, or possibly some special healing energy inherent in these "power places." If an unusual cure were to occur unexpectedly in a place not known for its healing effects, one would have to say that belief played no part. To my knowledge, a remote cave in the Kalahari desert has never been ascribed these properties by the San or any other of the local peoples. This story is about that cave.

Inner Passages, Outer Journeys[4] describes the unique healing properties of nature and the importance of wilderness and wild places as ideal environments for wellness and healing. Encountering nature means dealing with numerous disparities, the balance of which leads to wholeness. The root of all colors, shades of light, sounds, smells, tastes, feelings, and vibrations can be found in the wild. Nature is aroma and sound therapy all at once. A babbling brook or the whisper of the wind may be more potent than any mantra, and the smells and scents nature provides more wonderful than any incense. Nature is the ultimate repository for all incongruities and reinforces the core truth of the vitality associated with

balancing the opposites. If we go into the wilderness, as enlightened sages have done for millennia, one moment we may be lost
but the next we may be found. We may freeze, but when the sun
comes out on a high mountain pass, we are warm again; we may
be starving and then stuffed, thirsty and dehydrated and then
quenched, calm and then terrified, up and then down. Nature
teaches us that there can be no pleasure without pain, no rose
without thorns. We connect with our inner being when we
become one with the rhythms of the cosmos—sun energy, moon
energy, tides, seasons, daily and monthly cycles. The ability of the
San to control etheric energy is testament to the transcendental
alchemy that results from prolonged and intimate exposure to
wild places.

Some years ago I took a trip to the northwest of Botswana, to
a place where the San Bushmen still practice their trance dance. I
had marveled at this phenomenon for many years, even as a child
when learning about it at school. More recently, my interest had
deepened because of its close connection to the Kundalini experience of the Yogis, as well as its relevance as an original core model
for healing. I was anxious to witness this primal energy in the
remote Kalahari desert.

My older son, Terry, and I took off from Maun in a four-wheel
drive Toyota Hilux. Little did we realize the adventure that await-
ed us. Our rudimentary map provided directions. It took us nearly two days of intense driving along a soft, sandy track to reach
our destination. As we got closer, we started to encounter more
San people living in the area.

The Bushmen, or San, are the last hunter-gatherers of Africa.
More than ten years ago, it was estimated that there were about
60,000 San still living in the Kalahari, and fewer than 1,000 living
in an almost Stone Age existence as their ancestors did.[5] There are
far fewer living this way today. In fact, the few San who hold to
the old traditions still need to live in two worlds to survive. They
flip-flop between the more contemporary Kalahari and their
ancient hunter-gatherer way of life.

The San have different physical features from their Bantu neighbors. They are short of stature, have copper-colored skin, peppercorn hair, and delicate facial features. They have slanting eyes and high cheek bones, with more of a mongoloid than a negroid appearance.

As we approached a small encampment, we noticed a San man sitting under the shade of an acacia tree. When we asked him where we could find Royal (the San man who was to be our interpreter), he seemed to understand immediately and indicated that he would be able to help us. He jumped into the Hilux, seated himself between Terry and me, and pointed in a westward direction.

Eventually we reached a fence, which was the Namibian border. I had no idea we were so close to the perimeter, and when our friend beckoned that we should cross the fence over a convenient style (ladder-like steps leading over the top of the fence and down the other side), I became dubious about the whole undertaking. We were puzzled and perplexed, but the man was adamant, and we thought Royal might be on the other side of the fence visiting a relative or two. I looked around, but all I could see was the vast Kalahari Desert. There was nothing else visible; everything was still and silent—which should have warned me. We decided to cross over and find Royal.

The minute we climbed over the fence I had a sickening feeling of foreboding. I turned around and was confronted by four fully-armed Botswana soldiers who appeared out of the bushes on the Botswana side. Terry, the San man, and I, however, were now firmly ensconced on the Namibian side, and there was no doubt that we had done something terribly wrong.

The corporal in charge of the small group rapidly made it clear that we were in serious trouble, and after we crossed back onto the Botswana side he instructed us to come with him into the bush. One of the soldiers took a bandoleer of bullets and loaded it into his machine gun. In that instant, I was quite sure we were going to be shot and no one would be any the wiser. I suggested that we remain with the vehicle, but we were encouraged to move in the opposite direction, which we intuited by a change in the attitude of their weapons. Eventually, after walking a short distance, we were left in the shade of a thorn tree with armed guards while the corporal went off to find his superiors.

Shortly before we arrived in the country, we had been told some gruesome stories of what had happened to unruly tourists in Botswana. With these stories in mind, we sat underneath an acacia tree anticipating the verdict.

A lieutenant arrived and I tried to explain that I had come to visit the Kung San to observe their healing techniques. When I had crossed the border I thought it was a game fence; there are many of these fenses in Botswana to prevent wildlife from migrating into agricultural and cattle areas, and, likewise, to prevent cattle and goats crossing into wilderness and game reserves. However, according to the Botswana Defense Force (B.D.F.), we were criminals who had crossed an international border illegally, and we were going to suffer the consequences.

The lieutenant informed me, after hearing all the evidence, that we were lucky not to be shot, and that we would spend at least fourteen days in a Botswana jail to clear our senses. Even if our stories were true, ignorance was no excuse. He told me we would be interrogated by his commanding officer, after which we would be interred. We were to follow him in his Land Rover.

A soldier jumped in the back of the vehicle I was to drive, as the lieutenant raced off in his Land Rover at breakneck speed. I kept far enough back from his vehicle, which resembled a cloud of dust, so I could see the track more clearly and avoid the thorn trees, as well as the aardvark holes and the giant ant heaps. After a few minutes of traveling like this, he stopped, got out of his car, and furiously came up to me. He thrust his hand through the window and grabbed my shirt, screaming, "You are not driving fast enough!" Anxious not to displease him further, I sped up. Dust or not, I put my foot down flat and literally tailgated him through the Kalahari at lunatic speed, managing by the grace of some hidden power to avoid the obstacles in my way. When we arrived, the lieutenant glanced at me fleetingly and remarked, "That was better!"

Nevertheless, things went from bad to worse as we met up with his commander. After the lieutenant summarized the situation, we were faced with the commander's fury. He accused us of being South African spies and said we would be treated appropriately.

After repeating my defending statement for the last time to the commander, I added that I was clearly at the wrong place at the wrong time. It was only when I said this that the mood lightened, and they all agreed with me and laughed. I had scored points on at least two accounts. One was my ability to keep up with the lieutenant, who was plainly trying to lose me with his superlative bush driving, and the second was my diverting comment. I felt the pressure beginning to ease, and there was some release in the tense atmosphere. The commander said something to the lieutenant in Setswana which I could not understand, but he seemed to ask if he thought we were telling the truth. By the nature of the lieutenant's demeanor as well as his body language, I gathered that he replied in the affirmative. They walked away, out of hearing distance, and upon returning, gave us back our passports and said they would trust us not to leave until they received a directive from the authorities in Gaberones in the morning.

The next morning, they informed us we were not allowed to remain in the area but we were free to return to Maun and then home. As a concession, they allowed us to go by way of Xai Xai and the Gcwihaba caves, which I had been told were worth a visit. The stretch of road to Xai Xai was the worst yet, but Terry drove like an expert. We had no sooner escaped one difficulty when I was presented with another: I noticed with alarm that my uvula (the small fleshy projection at the back of the throat) had swollen to gigantic proportions and seemed to be sticking at the back of my palate. I was having great difficulty swallowing my saliva, and I was worried that if it grew any bigger I might have trouble breathing. I kept looking at my throat intermittently in the car mirror as Terry drove, wondering what had caused the swelling.

Months later, I asked an ear, nose, and throat surgeon about the incident, and he suggested that it might have been a streptococcal infection. My explanation was somewhat different. I had been eating and breathing dust for two days and talking incessantly to extricate us from a tough situation. Added to this, I was considerably stressed by the prospect of being responsible for getting my son shot. This swelling is sometimes described as an angioneurotic edema, which means the mechanism of the swelling has a lot to do with the blood vessels and nerves. I could not help but think that in my instance the emphasis must have been on the "neurotic" or nerve-induced component.

En route, we picked up two San men who wanted to return to Xai Xai. We dropped off one passenger close to Xai Xai and continued onto Gcwihaba with the other, Ke'eme, who was happy to take us to the caves. Approximately one hour out of Xai Xai, we came across the Gcwihaba, which was recognizable only by the end of the dirt track, a small outcrop of rocks, and an inconspicuous sign that was mostly obscured by bushes. The initial impression was extremely deceptive, and it was only after one climbed down into an amphitheater that the magnificent underground cavern revealed itself. With the help of Ke'eme, we planned to traverse the caves, which we entered in the west and were to exit from an opening in the east.

All this time I was quite concerned about the swelling in the back of my throat, since the fine-textured powdery dirt in the cave kicked up when we walked. I could see a veil of dust in the beam of the flashlight. With a bandanna covering my nose, I started to ascend a long, narrow, vertical chimney. I had the misgiving that maybe I would not make it through if there was any impairment of my breathing. An earlier explorer had left a rope to help climbers make their way to the top, and a strange thing happened as I climbed. There was a sense of peace and calm—a knowing that the back of my throat was going to be fine by the time I left the caves. No sooner had we climbed up the chimney and out the east exit of the caves than this proved to be true. I was astounded. Something strange had happened in the chimney, possibly some medicine power granted to me by a San ancestral spirit who had determined that I already had suffered enough.

We decided to go back to the village of Xai Xai to spend the night, and, if possible, witness a trance dance before our return to Maun. It was a school holiday weekend in Xai Xai, and Jackie, one of the schoolteachers, suggested we sleep inside one of the classrooms. This was just as well, since a cold front was coming through and in the next few days temperatures dropped precipitously.

The next day was cold and windy, though the sun shone brilliantly. My overriding motivation was still to see a healing dance. I asked Jackie to find out if there would be one that night. We returned to the school after an exploration of the area with one of the Kung hunters. Jackie informed us there would be a dance, and two of the primary healers who lived close to the chief's hut would attend.

The three of us set off to witness the healing dance of the San Bushmen under a full moon in the brilliant Kalahari sky. There were eight females and two male dancers, who were wearing rattles bound around their ankles. The females chanted, clapped, and sang, while the two men danced around the small fire. We were later told that one of the men was the most powerful dancer in the area. He carried a zebra-tailed whisk which he moved rhythmically as he danced; he was a vigorous and beautiful dancer and, as is customary with experienced dancers, he did not take much time to enter a trance. The second man looked as if he needed healing himself. He had a hacking cough and moved with more of a limp than a dance. In earlier days he had been a powerful healer.

The night was startling in its clarity and coldness. I could understand why, in winter, it was good if the dancers tranced quickly, while in summer everyone was happy to go on all night. Naturally, the near-naked dancers were protected from the cold, first by the exercise and later by the trance itself, which generates tremendous inner heat.

When the trance came, the dancer reeled and stumbled and had to sit down in a loose squat, sometimes with arms stretched out behind to hold him upright. He did not seem to care where he sat, and frequently one of the women would gently push him away from the fire. At one time his feet landed in the coals before they were nudged out by one of the women. I later examined his foot and found no sign of a burn. Following this, he went around the circle to each one in turn, laying on hands, and exorcising any disease he saw. He laid hands on Terry and me on a few occasions, and later, after the trance, he indicated that we were both healthy and not in need of healing. Jackie kept us informed throughout the dance as to what was happening.

When it came time for the healing of the second dancer, who was known to be ill, the first dancer continued to trance. This was a bad prognostic sign according to Jackie, no doubt because of the prolonged negotiation that was going on between the healer and the ancestral spirits on behalf of the patient. Apparently, the spirits had indicated that this particular man could no longer be helped, and that it was likely they would shortly take him over, onto their side.

Not even healing is taken too seriously by the San, and there was a lot of joking, laughter, and teasing directed at the healer, who was drowsy as he emerged from his trance-like state. Apparently, this was a result of Jackie's chiding him about his testicle, which was poking out of his loin cloth. She kept pointing to it with her finger.

We drove back to the schoolyard in the Hilux, feeling light-hearted. We had witnessed the ecstatic dance at the end of our long ordeal and we felt comforted by the fact that we were both well and healthy. We were sad for the healer who was ill and was soon to join the ancestors. My throat had now recovered completely, and I was confident that the circumstances surrounding the swelling were so unusual that it was unlikely to recur. I was wrong.

A few years later, I had another episode that followed a visit to Montana for a meeting. There, I gave two workshops of one-and-a-half hours each, on two consecutive days; so again, excessive talking appeared to be a precipitating factor. Within my civilized surroundings, I felt sure that an antihistamine tablet and a good dose of antibiotic, in case it was a streptococcal infection, would take care of the swelling in no time. Needless to say, six hours later I was worse, and the size of the uvula in the back of my throat was as great as I remembered seeing it in the Hilux mirror while driving through the Kalahari dust. I visited a colleague who gave me a heavy dose of antihistamine and a potent antibiotic in the rump. I took another dose of antibiotic and more antihistamine an hour later, but in spite of all the drugs circulating in my blood stream, it was not until later that night that I experienced any relief. The next morning I was still swollen, although much improved.

All I can say is that a single dose of a brief sojourn in the tunnel of a dusty cave alleviated the same problem in a matter of minutes. Furthermore, this therapy withstood a dusty drive, a windy cold walk, and two freezing Kalahari nights sleeping on the concrete floor of a dirty school room. I cannot discount that the San shaman did some follow-up treatment the second night, but I believe he spoke the truth when he told me I was completely healthy. Certainly, the minute I left the cave I had felt as good as new. Since that time I fully accept the notion that certain places are endowed with unique healing qualities.

NOTES

1. Cumes, David. *Inner Passages, Outer Journeys.* St. Paul, Minnesota: Llewellyn Publications, 1998.

2. Kaplan, Rachel, and Stephen Kaplan. *The Experience of Nature.* New York: Cambridge University Press, 1989.

3. Cumes, *Inner Passages, Outer Journeys.*

4. Ibid.

5. Van der Post, Laurens and Jane Taylor. *Testament to the Bushmen.* London: Penguin, Rainbird Publishing Group, 1984.

KUNDALINI, NUM, AND THE TREE OF LIFE

Whatever we see or don't see, whatever exists, right from the earth to the sky is nothing but Kundalini. It is the supreme energy which moves and animates all creatures, from the elephant to the tiniest ant.

—Swami Muktananda

I feel myself again. I feel my body and my flesh properly. Num makes your heart sweet.

—Description of the trance dance by San shaman to Richard Katz

I invite you to go on a journey to distant lands where healing is done in a different way. Imagine yourself in the interior of the Kalahari desert. You are a visitor to a group of Kung San and have come to observe their ancient healing techniques. One night you are sitting around the fire and the women gathered around start to clap and chant. The men wrap rattles around their legs and begin to dance. You and the breathtaking Kalahari sky are the only other witnesses to an amazing dance that is about to unfold. After a short time, one of the dancers staggers, shakes, and falls. You look into his eyes and all you can see is a vacant stare. The shaman's soul has

85

left the body and is soaring into the world of ghosts and ancestral spirits. Later, you learn that on this occasion he entered the home of the Great Spirit with great trepidation to plead for the life of a child who is dying. When his spirit is ready to return from this near-death, the women help the re-entry by massaging the body of the healer with warm sand. The shaman now circles the group and, with his new knowledge, divines the source of disease among the clan. He lays on hands and rubs sweat into the bodies of those who are ailing. He spends a much longer time with the child who is lying motionlessly under a cover of skins. After the laying on of hands, he shakes his fists at the heavens and shouts and screams at the Milky Way, exorcising the infirmities. The dance dwindles and stops shortly before sunrise. Later the following afternoon, the child sits up and for the first time in days asks for some food. You are still trying to figure out how this shaman could have had his foot in the fire without showing any sign of being burned.

Now you are in the icy mountains of Tibet. You have been told there are Yogis here who are able to sit naked, covered with wet sheets that they dry by generating inner heat. You have come to confirm this remarkable talent of energy control, which you have been told is related to the Kundalini serpent energy. After Tibet, you travel to the icy peak of Coyariti in Peru. Here you observe healers who have completed an all-night vigil on the frozen glacier. They have carved out large blocks of ice to take to their villages. They carry the blocks the next day—all day—on their backs. Miraculously, most do not suffer the consequences of lethal hypothermia, even with their seemingly scant clothing.

To complete your healing quest you travel to the jungles of the Amazon, where you participate in an ancient healing ceremony. You drink a potion of Ayahuasca, the vision vine of the jungle. You are astounded by the accuracy with which the shaman diagnoses your complaint; something you have not yet vocalized. He lays on hands and blows sacred smoke all over you. You return home, confused, but feeling healthier than you can ever remember. You learn that there are also powerful shamans in the desert regions of Peru who use a different hallucinogen, the San Pedro cactus, to access the same healing magic.

All these phenomena are related in that they illustrate different ways of awakening the feminine Shakti power and precipitating the diverse manifestations of Kundalini energy. These deeper states of awareness, or expanded states of consciousness, have been credited first and foremost to the Hindu and Yogi traditions. Advanced Yogis were able to move the magical feminine Shakti along an energy hierarchy up the vertebral column. When this Shakti, Kundalini, or serpent power, which arises from the base of the spine, meets the masculine, or Shiva principle, which resides just above the crown of the head, the Yogi experiences ecstasy or Samadhi. The Yogis call the primal, feminine energy of the cosmos the Kundalini, the San call it Num. The Yogis name their ecstatic experience Samadhi, the San call it Kia. The Yogis were aware of this phenomenon several thousand years ago, but the San painted it on the rocks of their continent possibly as long as 30,000 years ago.[1,2]

The San do not use hallucinogens, but are able to enter profoundly altered states of consciousness because of a finely tuned awareness resulting from their hunter-gatherer existence in the Kalahari wilderness. San shamans are renowned for their extraordinary powers of divination and healing, which they manifest through the trance dance. There are many non-San people in the Kalahari—black and white—who would sooner see a San healer than their own medicine person.

No matter what technique is used by the healer, there is a certain universal truth that must be applied. This core belief of balancing the opposites to achieve equilibrium has been known for eons, and we must beware that this truth is not put aside and forgotten because of the seduction and marvels of modern technology.

The San's healing abilities are peerless because of their hunter-gatherer lifestyle, which embraces all the polarities of nature.

Although these healers cannot read or write, their ability to balance the opposites encountered in the wild Kalahari gives them unrivaled control of healing energy. The San's ability to heal cannot be separated from their sense of place, the Kalahari desert in which they live and the diverse polarities they contend with to survive from day-to-day. They are constantly juggling the opposites that nature provides: hunger and fullness, the scorching daytime heat and the cold of the desert night, fear and tranquillity, light and dark, and so on. In fact, the yoga notion of sun and moon is germane to the San.[3] Buddha also emphasized the importance of the middle way, and this understanding occurred after prolonged contemplation and meditation in nature.

The San are close to the elements, and this intimacy may help them with the alchemy needed to transform their energy centers—the lower five of which are associated with an element. The fact that, unlike the hunter-gatherers of the Amazon, the San can do this without hallucinogens is all the more remarkable—nor do they have any of the esoteric techniques of yoga to induce the state, such as meditation, breath control, and sensory withdrawal. Those who are interested in the mechanisms of healing can aspire to their advanced intuitive, diagnostic, and therapeutic abilities, which arise out of the softer approach of tapping into the more feminine, right-brain dimension, not only of themselves, but also of the earth mother and the cosmos. This could be the reason why the women are able to trance more easily than the men, require only a brief apprenticeship, and often are the best healers.

This ability to move the spirit that heals has probably existed as long as humans have walked the planet, and we need to familiarize ourselves with its mechanism. The Hindu Kundalini and the anatomy and bioenergetic behavior of chakras and their energy channels lie at the core of healing. Balancing these forces empowers the healer and the Inner Healer of the patient as well. It also facilitates access to the "Field" and, therefore, is vital to the four variables of healing.

The Kung concept of disease is that "sickness" (or imbalance) resides in everyone, but only manifests in some as illness or disease.[4] Their healing, or trance dance, is thought not only to cure disease, but also to prevent imbalance (sickness) from developing into disease or illness by harmonizing the group. It is an advanced form of preventative health care that goes to the source of all afflictions. This occurs because everyone in the group experiences some balancing of their energy body and their inner being.

Num lies dormant at the base of the spine and in the pit of the stomach. During the dance, the Num energy intensifies as the singing and clapping increase. As Num travels up the spine to the crown, Kia occurs. The healers then travel into the spirit world, or the heavens, to entreat and argue with the ancestral spirits and the Great Spirit for the patient's health. As Num induces Kia, the healers may scream in pain, become stiff, convulse, stagger, and fall. They sweat profusely and may have a blank stare. When they return from the out-of-body experience, the shamans approach members of the clan, lay on hands, pull out the infirmity, and shake their hands toward the heavens, casting out any illness into the darkness.

The San believe that Num was given to the San Bushmen by the spirits. Those who can heal possess Num. Num heats up and becomes a vapor, a description similar to that of the yoga tradition, where the vibrational change causes an elemental shift from earth to water to fire to air to ether as energy moves up the chakras. One of the San shamans, when interviewed by Richard Katz,[5] an anthropologist who has studied the dance, drew the Num energy as a zigzag line traveling up the center of the body. Similar representations can be seen in the ancient rock art of the San. As this vibrational energy rises up the spinal column, the spine tingles. Descriptions of the trance dance given to Katz by healers[6] included a feeling of becoming oneself again, unfolding, unwinding, untying oneself, spreading oneself apart, or feeling oneself. All of these accounts have some of the attributes of Samadhi, or bliss or unity consciousness. Similarly, in the Tree of Life of Jewish mystical Kabbalah, the highest sephira, Keter the crown, is the place of "I am that I am."[7] In the state of Kia, the San shaman too comes into recognition of the true or higher Self.

The complex sounds of the San's chants are vital in transporting the spirit to other worlds, and probably incorporate all of the qualities of primordial sound so vital to the Yogi, who can move Kundalini energy. The Kundalini is thought by the Hindus to be the origin of primordial sound, which has the capacity to favorably influence and align our energy body. To the San, singing is felt to be critical to the whole process—if it decreases or stops, the Num falls off drastically. Num songs help the healer raise Num up the spine so Kia can occur. The chanting, singing, and clapping is unlike any other music and, in the context of the Kalahari night and the flickering primal fire, has tremendous power. San healers are well aware of the importance of the women in generating the energy of the dance with this unique form of sound. Similarly, the Ayahuasca shamans of the Amazon recognize the importance of Icaros, or sacred chants, in amplifying the effect of the hallucinogen Ayahuasca in their healing ceremonies.

If we are to make sense of these experiences, we need to understand them in the light of a different model of healing than that delineated by modern Western allopathic medicine. If we look at ancient texts, we can see that thousands of years ago the Yogis described an anatomical and physiological energy body unknown to modern medicine. This psycho-spiritual model seems universal, even though the details may vary. The phenomenon is common to Tibetan Buddhism, Chinese Taoism, some Native North American traditions, and the San.

The similarities between Kundalini and Num have been outlined previously. Descriptions of the energy anatomy of the chakras and the pathways that emanate from them are also summarized in *Inner Passages, Outer Journeys*[8] and detailed in numerous other texts.[9,10] An understanding of this system is vital to the "Spirit of Healing." Both Num and Kundalini can lead to magical powers. In the case of the San, this enables them to see "into" people and diagnose illness.

Briefly, there are seven main chakras, or "wheels" of energy, situated along the spinal axis; the first begins at the coccyx and the seventh ends above the crown. There are at least 72,000 energy channels along which the life force, or prana, travels. The three most important channels travel up the spinal axis. These are the moon channel, the sun channel, and the central channel.

The moon channel representing the feminine is cool, blue, and contracts or restrains. The sun channel portrays the masculine force—it is red, hot, and expands. The sun and moon channels wind around the central channel helicly and meet at each chakra. The central channel begins at the base and runs up the axis of the spine to the crown. This is the pathway for the sacred Shakti, or feminine Kundalini energy. The Kundalini lies dormant in the central column at the base of the spine, in the first chakra, and is represented symbolically by an archetypal serpent which is wound around the central channel.

Usually the life force (prana) moves up and down the sun and moon pathways, leading to our normal state of perception. With special inner practices, this vital internal energy can be directed into the central channel causing stimulation of the Kundalini, which resides there and expands the level of consciousness. As this vibrational energy ascends the chakra ladder, it heats up and eventually becomes a vapor. There is an elemental change in the hierarchy of chakras as earth changes to water, to fire, to air, and finally to ether. This does not seem entirely incredulous, since if we examine our bodies subatomically, the particles are not only moving but are surrounded by expanses of empty space. It is possible that as the vibrational energy increases, the shaman becomes immune to the effects of scorching heat, since the vibrating frequency of this micromatter is now the same as that of the flames. Certainly, control of heat is a spectacular manifestation of this magical state. This could also explain how Tibetan Yogis and mountain shamans can generate inner heat and are immune to the effects of freezing temperatures. Consciousness appears to control the vibrational energy in our cells.

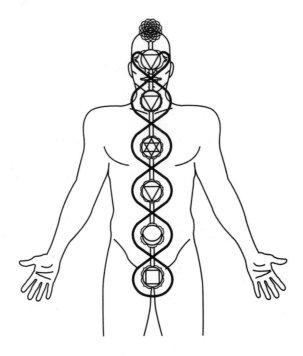

The Chakra System

When polarity balance in the sun and moon helix occurs, energy is directed into the central column. This awakens the sleeping serpent, or Shakti energy, and the Kundalini rises up the central column. If the serpent power is fully activated, it ascends, charging and energizing each chakra as it goes. Should the female

Shakti energy rise up all the way to the seventh, or crown chakra, it will meet with Shiva, the male principle. When Shakti and Shiva meet at the crown's 1,000 petal lotus, Samadhi, transcendence, or contact with the higher Self, occurs. Here, the individual Self dissolves, and the observer, the observed, and the process of observing become fused into one. Even greater magical and medicinal powers occur in this space, where all sense of duality disappears and the Yogi attains unity consciousness.

The sixth chakra, or third eye, is behind and between the eyes. Here lies our intuitive awareness, or ability to have paranormal powers and clairvoyance. This chakra represents the sixth sense, so important to the skill of any medical intuitive or shaman. Once the Kundalini has risen this far, our inherent magical powers are potentiated.

Researchers[11,12,13] have done studies to verify whether there is any scientific basis to the chakra system, and were able to show that there is some foundation for its existence. Using electrodes, they were able to measure electrical potentials arising from the chakras. Observing experienced meditators, psychics appointed by the research team confirmed that the meditators were able to project energy out of their chakras, and the color changes in those chakras correlated exactly with the wave patterns of the electrical recordings taken from those chakras. Each color specific to a particular chakra that was noted in the auric field of the subject was associated with a different electrical wave shape and frequency. The chakras frequently carried the colors that had been described in the classical, metaphysical texts, for example, Kundalini red, heart green, throat blue, third eye violet, and crown white. It is likely that, as technology develops and we are able to measure the subtle energy fields more accurately, the mysticism of today will become the science of tomorrow.

The key to moving the Kundalini energy upward is the balance of the female and male energies, the cool moon and the hot sun. This bears a strong resemblance to the Western psychological approach of balancing the right-brain (feminine) or left-brain (masculine) to achieve whole brain function.

For the Kundalini to rise, the Yogi must go beyond the constraints of ego. The ego is the greatest hindrance to the upward movement of Kundalini. Another block to the flow of spiritual energy is a "knot" at the heart chakra. The San agree that the heart needs to be open for Num energy to flow freely.[14] Both yoga[15,16] and San traditions used psychedelic plants to open the heart, transcend ego, and introduce neophytes to the mystical realms, but cultural and traditional support for healing uses of these hallucinogens is absent in the West.

Although different shamans use their own techniques, the ability to move Kundalini energy is central to all these practices. The shaman must move the energy up to the third eye, or sixth chakra, for diagnostic and therapeutic clairvoyance. Furthermore, in order to travel out-of-body and navigate the cosmic realms, the energy must move into the seventh chakra. In this way, shamans obtain assistance from the spirit world and the Great Spirit for the sake of their patients. Anyone who can harness this energy to benefit fellow humans is likely to have amazing healing abilities; however, the same energy can be abused and cause harm.

Light experiences are part of the Kundalini phenomenon and lead to observations of inner light, light emanating from people such as the Buddha or Christ, and seeing lightning, illumination, or clear light. This may have led to the confusing descriptions by Peruvian Andean shamans of being initiated, or "struck," by a bolt of lightning. This may be true in the figurative rather than the physical sense. The Kabbalah talks of the lightning bolt that occurs if energy moves along the Tree of Life. San woman describe Num energy as moving like lightning.[17]

Having the ability to move the Kundalini up the chakras and align the energy body perfectly does not mean we can cure our current afflictions or prevent others from arising. Enlightened masters who have reached these higher vibrational states are not beyond illness. We have to conclude that even if we were spiritually advanced and in full control of our chakras, our understanding of the human condition, in health or in sickness, is far from complete. However, taking care of our energy bodies as well as our physical bodies by some sort of inner practice is surely a salutary start to a healing practice. Any attempt to increase the balance in this system is worthwhile. We cannot expect to be master adepts like the San without a lot of dedication.

If we define harmony and healing as the deep inner peace that occurs with the attainment of equilibrium within our energy system, then we do not need to be cured to be healed. One can have inner peace in the face of illness—this is the ultimate challenge to the patient, especially those with an incurable disease. Physicians have all seen patients with terminal conditions who cannot be cured but, by way of their equanimity, appear to be fully healed.

From the perspective of the healer, those who can move Kundalini energy are likely to be more effective with their intuitive and diagnostic abilities. They are also more powerful in inducing the Inner Healer of their patients to do its work.

Both patient and healer gain access to greater possibilities when they balance their energy bodies, move the Kundalini, and enter the Field.

The Tree of Life of Judaism is a different energy model with similar principles. Kabbalah affirms that it is our primary goal to re-enter Eden. In order to do this, we must conquer the snake—representative of ego—that is wound around the central pillar of the Tree of Life. By going beyond ego, we can re-enter the garden and recapture spiritual equanimity and physical balance. The Kabbalistic Tree of Life is an ancient archetype, another core model of opposites, and a means to return to Eden.

The Tree of Life is also a tool that both healer and patient can use in the healing process. The Tree assists both along the path to health and is also a doorway to the Field and to the Divine presence. Like the chakras and the Kundalini, the Tree of Life connects us to the four variables of the healing process.

The Tree of Life is composed of three limbs.[18,19] The key principle of the left limb is Rigor, the right, Mercy, and the middle, Will, which maintains the balance. On the left, Rigor represents passive force, constraint or constriction; on the right, Mercy confers the active force of expansion, and in the center, Will creates equilibrium.

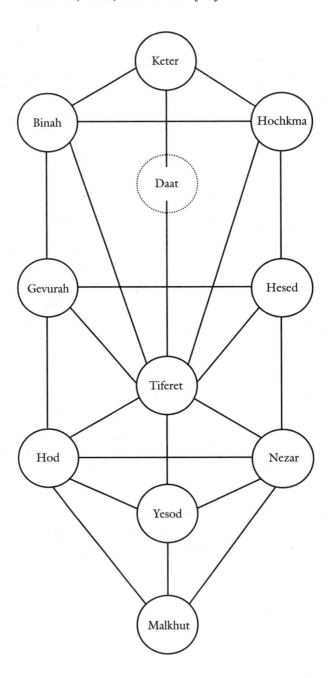

The Tree of Life

The Tree itself is composed of ten sephirot and twenty-two pathways between the sephirot. These sephirot are centers of force or energy, and are in some ways similar to the chakras in yoga. The crown or topmost sephira, Keter, is equivalent to the seventh chakra, the crown chakra, and represents all that was, is, and will be; "I am that I am." At Keter we come in direct contact with the higher Self, or that part of our being that is the essence of God.

The left pillar of the Tree is feminine, passive, receptive, watery, and blue in color. It is similar to the moon channel in yoga. The Kabbalists call this feminine force the Queen. In medical terms, it is analogous to the parasympathetic nervous system, which inhibits and constricts. For instance, the parasympathetic system is responsible for slowing down the heart rate and constricting the pupil.

The right-hand pillar of the Tree is masculine, active, fiery, or red, and involves active expansion. It is similar to the sun channel in yoga and the sympathetic nervous system. The sympathetic system speeds up the heart and dilates the pupil; it is invoked during a flight or fight reaction. The Kabbalists call this masculine force the King.

Binah, at the top of the left limb of the Tree, represents receptive, reflective, or passive intellect or understanding. Contemporary neurophysiology would localize this characteristic to the right-brain, which is creative and intuitive. Hochkma, Binah's opposite on the right side of the Tree, denotes inner intellect or wisdom, and is comparable to the cognitive or intellectual left side of the brain. Neurophysiologists might say we have attained whole brain function when both the left and right—Binah and Hochkma—are operative, and we have achieved balance.

The central or main pillar of the Tree represents equilibrium, grace, and will, and is the balance between the left and the right. In yoga, its equivalent in the body would be the central channel.

Daat, which means knowledge, is just below Keter and is not a true sephira. This is where knowledge from God can enter directly, possibly in the form of grace (which may be highly relevant for spontaneous healing). We increase our health balance as we ascend the central pillar of the Tree.

Energy travels down the Tree, from Keter at the top, to Malkhut at the bottom, traveling from center to right to left, and continuing down in this order. In this way, we are propagated down the Tree to Malkhut, where we become manifest in human form. Alternatively, from the perspective of each individual's life process, energy can travel in the opposite direction, upward from Malkhut to left to right and so on, eventually ending up in Keter. If we can attain Keter, we regain Eden. Going downward, the energy is sometimes called the lightning bolt, due to its zigzag character and direction. Kabbalah confirms that potential vibrational energy is not only present in our bodies, but pervades the entire cosmos as well.

The lowest sephira of Malkhut is the kingdom. This represents nature and the purely physical aspect of the body. Just as yoga has the concept of Kundalini, or the female Shakti energy, Kabbalah has the concept of Shekhinah, the feminine aspect of the Divine. God, in Kabbalah, has its equivalent in Shiva, or the male principle, in yoga. The Shekhinah rests at Malkhut, the first sephira, just as the Kundalini or Shakti energy resides in the root or first chakra. Malkhut contains the four elements of earth, water, fire, and air. Although we may attribute physical health to this lower sephira, complete health must occur with balance at every level of the Tree. For most of us, however, it would be very difficult to ascend to higher levels up the Tree if we were affected in any way by ill health. Therefore, attention to the basic elements of Malkhut is a necessary first step along the pathway.

Kabbalah affirms our aspiration to return to Eden from whence we came. It is the equivalent of the search for the higher Self of the Yogi. According to Kabbalah, the student must conquer the snake around the central trunk of the Tree in order to attain Keter, or enlightenment, much in the way that the Yogi must harness the Kundalini power to reach Samadhi.

The numerous components and polarities of the Tree of Life are all present in the original prototype of Adam and Eve in the

Garden of Eden, and also within each one of us. The Tree is a map to help us wend our way back to our birthright by helping us attain the necessary balance. Pristine wilderness can be a surrogate for Eden. Nature, especially, or any sacred place or space, along with the Tree, can help us identify and prevail over the complex challenges of life and health. Like the chakra energy system, the Tree can help the healer and patient access the Field and expand their potential to heal. An understanding of the polarities inherent in the Tree also lays the foundation for a concept of health balance that follows in chapter 10—a Tree of Health.

NOTES

1. Katz, Richard. *Boiling Energy*. Cambridge, Massachusetts: Harvard University Press, 1982.

2. Cumes, David. *Inner Passages, Outer Journeys*. St. Paul, Minnesota: Llewellyn Publications, 1998.

3. Ibid.

4. Katz, *Boiling Energy*.

5. Ibid.

6. Ibid.

7. Ibid.

8. Cumes, *Inner Passages, Outer Journeys*.

9. Johari, Harish. *Chakras: Energy Centers of Transformation*. Vermont: Destiny Books, 1987.

10. Mookerjee, Ajit. *Kundalini: The Arousal of Inner Energy*. London: Thames and Hudson, 1989.

11. Brennan, Barbara Ann. *Hands of Light*. (Summary of work by Valery Hunt, UCLA 1977, and Dr.Hiroshi Montoyama, Tokyo, Japan I.A.R.P., 1979.) New York: Bantam Books, 1987.

12. Gerber, Richard, M.D. *Vibrational Medicine*. Chapter 4 summary of work by Montoyama and Bentov. Santa Fe, New Mexico: Bear & Co., 1988.

13. Hunt, Valery, et al. Abstract. "A study of structural integration from neuromuscular, energy field and emotional approaches." Sponsored by the Rolf Institute of Structural Integration, 1977.

14. Katz, *Boiling Energy*.

15. Feuerstein, Georg. *Yoga: The Technology of Ecstasy*. Los Angeles: Jeremy P. Tarcher, Inc., 1989.

16. Feuerstein, Georg. *The Encyclopedic Dictionary of Yoga*. New York: Paragon House, 1990.

17. Katz, Richard, Megan Biesele and Verna St. John. *Healing Makes Our Hearts Happy*. Rochester, Vermont: Inner Traditions, 1996.

18. Ben Shimon, Halevi Zev. *Kabbalah Tradition of Hidden Knowledge*. London: Thames and Hudson, 1992.

19. Epstein, Pearl. *Kabbalah, The Way of the Jewish Mystic*. Boston, MA: Shambhala, 1972.

SOUL LOSS OR LOSS OF SELF—A DISEASE OF OUR TIMES

To know the real Self to be one's own is the greatest attainment according to the scriptures and reasoning. To know the non-self such as the ego, to be the Self is no attainment at all. One should therefore renounce this misconception of taking the non-self for the Self.

—Sri Sankarcharya

To be truly balanced and whole, the patient needs to be connected with Self. Ancient wisdom teaches us that ego and Self are almost mutually exclusive. The more the ego, the less we are in contact with the higher Self. In fact, they are inversely proportional. If we can minimize ego, Self emerges. According to Eastern tradition, this dictum is as sure as the law of gravity. If we jump from the second floor of a building we will have to contend with the impact of our body on the ground below. If we nurture ego, we will have to face the issue of deprivation of Self. If we need to come into alignment with our higher, or true Self, for more complete healing, what happens if we neglect to do so and are disconnected from Self? If there is disparity between our soul's or Self's purpose in the universe, this will manifest initially as unhappiness and disharmony, and later as physical pathology as well. This separation will be experienced as Self or soul loss.

In medical texts, diseases are always broken down and classified into sections so that the complexities can be more easily studied. Physicians are accustomed to talking about disease under titles such as: cause or etiology, incidence, pathology, treatment, or prognosis. This classification will be used in this chapter for the sake of convenience. There is no medical text today that would describe the condition of soul loss. Yet, this affliction may be the foundation for many of the maladies we see in our modern world. As the science and spirituality of medicine becomes more integrated, we may yet see this "dis-ease" described.

DEFINITION

There are many esoteric methods for making contact with Self. Eastern traditions and Western psychologists like Carl Jung and Abraham Maslow have said that the drive toward the real, true, or higher Self is at the root of all human motivation. This is what is moving us subconsciously, and it is omnipresent whether we realize it or not. Jung described the term persona (mask) to represent that part of ourselves with which we outwardly identify. The persona and ego are acquisitive and relate to the material things that surround us. When it comes to possessions, ego (persona) never has enough, and when it gets more "things," it remains dissatisfied. According to Eastern scriptures, our self-grasping and self-cherishing wants are the source of much of our misery. Since ego is so unstable, it is easy to see how the Yogis thought it illusory. For us to reach the true Self, we have to go beyond persona or ego and become transpersonal. The real Self is stable and fixed; it just "is." Self represents pure being, and is there for its own sake without hidden agendas or ulterior motives. This true Self has other labels. If we were Christian we would call it the soul, or our Christ-like nature. Judaism refers to Self as that godlike part of ourselves. If we were Yogis, we would call this Atman, and if we were Buddhists, we would call it our Buddha nature. We need to go beyond ego in order to reach Self, and for this, we need awareness that ego is the greatest deterrent to the realization of

Self. Loss of Self is an ailment signifying a lack of connection with our higher Self, true Self, soul, or Atman, and can also be called soul loss or soullessness. This predicament arises from our being bound to the "yoke" of ego, and sages have warned us about the implications for eons. We need to subordinate the ego if we wish to reach for the higher purpose of connecting with Self. Jesus affirmed that "he who loses himself will find himSelf." In other words, those who lose their ego Self will find their higher Self. True inner healing occurs when we realize Self.

To a shaman, soul loss is a grave diagnosis and a major cause of illness and death. This condition, although not recognized by Western medicine, carries a poor prognosis to the shaman. Just as a major life crisis can lead to personal transformation by making us humble (subordinating ego) and forging a connection with the higher Self, it can also have the opposite effect and cause soul loss, cutting the afflicted party off from their own soul. The calamity strikes at the core of the person's being and can devastate the immune system, leading to cancer and other disease manifestations. Soul loss is not always so dramatic, but it can lead to a slow, insidious deterioration of the person's mental or inner health, which eventually will manifest itself physically. Western medicine cannot cure this malady. Alternative medicine, traditional shamanic techniques, and Jungian and transpersonal psychology can help. Since the problem occurs on the inside, one must go inward to deal with it.

CAUSE

The main cause of Self loss is misperception, or maya (illusion). Many of us are unaware that something lies beyond ego, and we confuse the little self with the big Self that lies beyond. We believe we are our ego and our persona, and since nothing satisfies the ego, this leads to suffering. Modern-day consumerism, materialism, and technology feed the ego, leading to separation from the true Self. According to Eastern philosophy, egocentricity leads to selfishness and desirous attachment, factors that hinder our spiritual development. Ego makes us judge others and believe we are better than they, reinforcing itself. Materialism and consumerism feed directly off our desire and attachment to things. Our Western predicament is a result of our culture's need to reinforce ego to maintain the continuation of our consumer society. The media is skilled in telling us that without a certain new product, our life may not be worth living. They sometimes couch this indoctrination in terms of religious and spiritual jargon to make us believe we may be making contact with a higher force in the process of acquiring something material. Some advertisements or commercials portray objects with a mystique that borders spuriously on the mystical and sacred. They are trying to connect us with an ego-driven want by dishonestly masquerading it in language representing Self. Our American dream will become a nightmare if unabashed materialism prevails, because it aggravates the condition of Self loss.

THE DEVELOPMENT OF SELF LOSS

The search for the true Self, or the higher Self, is a search for the divine. We all would like to have a direct experience of God, or at least a direct experience with that part of ourselves that is godlike or made in the image of God. The lack of this connection or the inability to do this results in Self loss. Our early development is wrapped up in developing the little self or ego. The related energy resides in the lower chakras, or those energy centers below the diaphragm. Our ego sense, our worldly power base, rests in the third chakra in the region of the solar plexus. Our inability to raise the energy above the third chakra and above the diaphragm, or above Yesod on the Tree of Life, is primarily responsible for our limited sense of Self. Most of us are content to do what society expects of us—to have a suitable profession or occupation, a nice house and car, and our kids in good schools. Add to this a healthy bank balance and a prosperous retirement plan, and we think we have it all. These qualities are inherent in the lower chakras and do not lead to inner peace. It is only when we raise the energy above the diaphragm into the upper chakras, or to the sephira of Tiferet on the Tree of Life, that we can develop more inner harmony and better health.

It is when we get beyond the physical body, which relates directly to the first three chakras, and move toward the center of our being that we have a hope of curing this condition of Self loss. Mind and ego are intimately connected, and if we can subordinate these to our higher wisdom with the help of some form of meditation or a Zenlike mindfulness, we may be able to reach expanded states of consciousness.

It is essential for us to first develop the ego part of ourselves. The first three chakras and the physical body cannot be ignored, and must be developed before moving upward. We cannot skip chakras; the necessary homework must be done with all requirements fulfilled. One has to have an ego in the first place before we can let it go.

Key to Self loss is the overemphasis of the importance of possessions, prestige, degrees, and titles. Ego reinforcing goal-orientated behavior is crucial to the attainment of material things, and is essential to the development of the third chakra. However, winning at work and at play can become pathological, making us egocentric and taking us out of contact with our true selves. According to Buddhist philosophy, awareness and knowledge of this basic spiritual truth are the antidote to desirous attachment and judgment, which feed our ego-grasping and self-cherishing nature.

We can look at the problem in psychological rather than mystical terms by referring to Maslow's model of the hierarchy of human needs.[1] He described two forms of need: Deficiency needs and Growth needs. Deficiency needs consist of the maintenance of stability, security, and protection. These are the needs that keep the supply lines open and regenerate the human species. They are invoked whenever a deficit is experienced and can only be laid aside once satisfied. These are also the needs residing in the lower three chakras. When they are fulfilled, we can begin to appreciate the Growth needs such as freedom, beauty, justice, and truth. Appreciation of these leads to self-actualization (being all that we can be), self-transcendence (i.e., transcendence of the ego-self), Self-realization, and peak experiences, the equivalent of contact with the higher Self. Maslow described the peak experience as a mystical event in which the individual transcends to clarity, euphoria, holism, and understanding, coming closer to the true Self and a sense of being. If we allow ourselves to believe that only Deficiency needs are important, we deviate from our calling, or truth in life. This can result in a lack of inner harmony and loss of Self.

MANIFESTATION

Self loss presents multiple manifestations including unhappiness, disharmony, agony, and torment. An individual or patient might appear to have everything, but is not satisfied. Other presentations vary and may reflect lethargy, depression, lack of energy, mood swings, weight gain, and reliving personal misery. Also prevalent are alienation from friends, family, children, and spouse, leading to separation, divorce, and family disintegration. According to Jung, turning to alcohol and drugs may be a distorted way of connecting with "Spirit."

The disease can span many age groups, but is more common after the age of forty. It is familiar to some as an existential or "midlife crisis." When this calamity strikes, patients come to realize that, in spite of material success, they are not happy. The condition seems more common in men than women, with burnout and fatigue syndromes occurring as frequent complications.

INCIDENCE

Except for a few enlightened individuals, we all suffer from Self loss to a greater or lesser degree because of the overwhelming influences of our "sophisticated" civilization. More primitive societies not exposed to the excesses of materialism may be spared from the epidemic. Unfortunately, they are soon "infect-ed" once contact with Western civilization is made. Those who believe they understand the mechanism of Self loss are just as much at risk as those who do not. The seduction of modern-day living is overwhelming. Even enlightened beings who acquire power may be overcome by ego and suffer a relapse. In this way many gurus fall into disrepute.

DIAGNOSIS

Those afflicted with Self loss live in a world of duality and separa-tion, believing that the persona and ego are the ultimate truth or reality. This duality leads to a constant differentiation between ourselves and "other," always to our own advantage and at the expense of "other." We alternate between pleasure and pain, try-ing as much as possible to hold on to those moments of joy and to avoid the periods of despair. We become beset with either hap-piness or distress, and have difficulty remaining in the middle path where neither gratification nor suffering have much emo-tional impact. Most of us who suffer from these emotional swings have not perfected a technique of going inward, or found a method for achieving inner peace. We remain goal-oriented and outwardly directed. Judgment of others, blame, recriminations, desire, and attachment for and to material possessions are hall-marks of the diagnosis. These characteristics exclude long-lasting equanimity.

TREATMENT

The primary treatment is knowledge of the truth, since "the truth will set us free." The key to this truth is self-awareness, the first step to self-transformation. Awareness can be developed by mind-fulness, being in the present moment, and meditation or some form of inner practice, either mental or physical. This will help us modulate mind and ego. As the San and the Yogis knew, opening the heart is the key to moving energy into the higher centers; the fourth chakra—love, tolerance, compassion, and empathy—are the gateway to the higher Self. The San are well aware that we frequently go out-of-balance and use the medium of their dance to bring their group back into alignment and harmony. The process is ongoing—it never stops. The San's practice is a physical one, made easy by the fact that they live in close harmony with nature. They have little need for esoteric mystical routines. The magic of the Kalahari and their hunter-gatherer lifestyle alone awakens awesome inner power. Their renewal with the dance can teach us important lessons. Just as we must clean, exercise, and feed our bodies on a regular basis, we need to be diligent with our spiritual maintenance as well.

There are many nondenominational tools that can be used to guide our path and help us turn inward. In addition to meditation and prayer, there are techniques such as yoga and tai chi. Wilderness and nature are also powerful instruments to help us go inward and connect with the true Self; the outer wilderness helps access the inner wilderness of the psyche. Nature can be used in many forms, and a regular garden practice may be just as useful as an infrequent backpacking trek.

Ego is always an impediment to transpersonal growth. A simple way to overcome its effect is to do everything for its own sake and not for any self-aggrandizing reason or goal. According to Eastern thought, it is ego-affirming behavior that leads us to accumulate bad karma—which is why we are born again and again. Our intention has everything to do with our actions, and if the intention is not pure and has an ulterior motive, the resultant action will have a profound affect on our spiritual progress, if not in a future life then at least in this one.

The inward bound path will nudge us gently, but painfully and slowly, toward the higher Self. This is where we find inner peace, and where judgment and desirous attachment have no place. Here, ego has no binding power over our actions and any activity is done for its own sake.

PROGNOSIS

If we ignore these principles from ancient wisdom and transpersonal psychology and become caught up in the trappings of Western materialism, the prognosis is poor. Yet self-awareness leading to self-treatment with different techniques tailored to one's individual preference can cure the condition of Self loss, or at least stop its progression. The process, however, is a continuous one, and a meaningful inner practice needs to be developed. We cannot rest on the laurels of past peak experiences, and should continually renew ourselves on the journey.

Ultimately, a connection with spirit leads to an alliance, not only with good mental and spiritual well-being, but with physical health as well. The paradox here is that if we are truly connected to Self, physical health becomes of secondary importance because we are now living in the realm of the higher chakras. This may be why illuminated beings sometimes disregard their physical health. Nevertheless, if we regard our body as a vehicle meant to carry us on life's journey, we must make sure the vehicle is in good order to complete it. However, from the point of view of patients who are incurably ill, they do not have to eliminate their disease to be "healed." Healing by realizing Self occurs at a much deeper level.

With work, we may be able to induce a complete remission of Self loss. Although this talk of spirit might disturb some as smacking of religion, healing also has to involve our inner being to be complete. Alliance with Self is the key to wholeness. If we can appreciate and acknowledge the importance of the hierarchy of chakras and strive to keep those energy wheels humming in harmony, and if we can realize the importance of what yoga philosophy, Kabbalah, and transpersonal psychology has to teach us, we will be on the way to a healthier life.

NOTES

1. Maslow, A. H. *The Farther Reaches of Human Nature*. New York: Penguin, 1976.

THE FIELD AND THE INNER HEALER

In a universe in which the consciousness of the physicist affects the reality of a subatomic particle, the attitude of a doctor affects whether or not a placebo works, and the mind of an experimenter affects the way a machine operates, we can no longer pretend that we are separate from that which we are studying.

—Michael Talbot[1]

Two essential factors that link to the Tree of Life need to be discussed before beginning to make a model for a Tree of Health. The first is the presence of an Inner Healer within all of us, and the second is the existence of a Field.

No one would doubt the beneficial affect of modern medical treatment such as drugs, antibiotics, chemotherapy, radiation therapy, or surgery. The same would hold true for traditional Eastern techniques like acupuncture and herbal medicines. However, we tend to forget that all these treatments are only assisting the Inner Healer of the patient, which is doing the work. Without the Inner Healer, no treatment would be effective. This is true for humans and animals.

Recently, my dog Tabi developed severe diabetes, which was difficult to manage even on high doses of insulin given twice a day. She developed a huge abscess on her abdomen and went into septic shock, which

111

required a visit to the vet to resuscitate her and drain the abscess. She was left with a huge gaping hole that seemed unlikely to heal, especially in view of the diabetes. She was doted on by my kids and given more love and attention than ever before. The vet suggested major surgery to close the defect, which seemed bound to fail because the area was infected. Some suggested we put her to sleep. No doubt because of all the love, devotion, and fuss, her Inner Healer said, "Heal!" This she did, in less than two weeks, and in spite of the difficulty in keeping the area clean. (Since it was impossible to monitor her all the time, she would lie with the open wound in the grass or dirt.) As healers with big egos, we would like to believe that we are responsible for our patients getting better. Herbalists would have attributed Tabi's quick and dramatic healing to the remedies they applied; homeopathists to their own particular concoction. A vet would have said it was the ideal combination of antibiotics, in light of a culture and sensitivity report from the bacteriologist. But in Tabi's case, her Inner Healer was responsible, because good diabetic control was absent and hygiene was far from optimal. The power of the Inner Healer in humans can be clouded by the medical profession taking credit for any favorable outcome.

We are less apt to appreciate the marvels of the Inner Healer at work because of therapeutic intervention. Healing without medical interference may take longer, but can nevertheless be spectacular. Recently, my yoga teacher approached me after class and asked me to check his armpit. There was a large mass of lymph glands present that was slightly tender. He had numerous scratches on his hands, possible entry sites for infection. The diagnosis seemed to be lymphadenitis, or infection in the lymph glands. He refused to take a course of antibiotics. I saw him a week later, and the mass was beginning to localize into an abscess. I felt reassured it was not a malignancy, and told him to come to the office in a few days where I would drain it for him. A week later, I went to Peru; on my return, he told me the abscess had ruptured, emitting a profuse volume of foul-smelling fluid, and after that all had been well. When the old medical text books described this as "laudable (praiseworthy) pus," they knew what they were talking about. The process, even if smelly, is beautifully designed, and his decision not to take the antibiotics and allow his Inner Healer to do the work proved to be correct. For eons, our Inner Healers have done quite well without the help of any formal interference.

The Inner Healer can be assisted by the placebo response, which occurs because of the belief of the patient in that medicine. Western medicine is well aware of the placebo effect. The belief that therapy can do something to cure a problem is so powerful that this faith has to be taken into account when evaluating the "actual effect" of different treatments. Whenever a treatment is evaluated, there is always a control group that is used to evaluate the placebo effect. A significant number of patients benefit when unknowingly given a dummy medicine. This is why some scientists are circumspect about nonallopathic healing. Claims for a cure may be a result of placebo rather than the influence of the medication itself. No one disputes that the power of placebo is a good thing, but medical science seeks to extract an additional benefit beyond the capacity of the Inner Healer alone. Many nonallopathic remedies have not withstood the scrutiny of a double blind study, and enthusiastic reports may be anecdotal. The interpretation of therapeutic results may also be suspect. If Tabi would had been given a powerful antibiotic during her convalescence, I may have been certain this was the reason for her rapid recovery. Western physicians, in their need to be scientific, would like to discount placebo when evaluating different treatments.

Western medicine has recently become aware of the objective benefits of therapeutic touch. Therapeutic touch specialists claim they can influence the healing process of the patient with or without direct physical contact. They claim that the healing comes from healing energy channeled through the healer. The healer, however, is in the immediate vicinity of the patient, and skeptics might attribute any change to the placebo effect. Alternatively, healing energy may traverse a space, or a Field, which in this case is only a small distance.

Whatever being comes to be, be it motionless or moving, derives its being from "field" and "knower of the field." Know this!
— *The Bhagavad-Gita*

Each one of us is a "knower" of the Field. Moreover, not only are we in the Field, but the Field is in us. The cosmic Field seems to extend from us as an energy reservoir in space through which signals pass back and forth. We could divide the messages that traverse the Field simply into Knowable and Unknowable. Light, sound, radio, TV, electromagnetic pulses, and chemicals as subtle as pheromones are some of the Knowable signals that travel through the Field.

Many Knowable "mini" fields are encountered in nature. We see it in the marvel of a termite colony, where the Field of intelligence of the colony far exceeds the capacity of the nervous system of any singular termite. Each individual member has its own particular place and fulfills a special role. The soldiers know what they have to do and the workers busy themselves relentlessly. The whole colony functions as an elaborate system, sending out relevant messages for every eventuality. All termites are interdependent—a lone termite cannot survive. As is the microfield of the termite colony, so is the macrofield of the cosmos. We can look around and see analogies in nature's complex ecosystems that are also part of the Field and governed by Divine intelligence or a higher force.

However, there are also Unknowable forces transmitted through the Field such as telepathic and healing energies, which science has been unable to define or measure. Most of us cannot communicate well with the Unknowable Field, but we can all learn to enter this dimension more effectively. Shamans, mystics, and enlightened beings have more intimate contact with this Field of possibilities.

When Einstein was asked about the nature of the cosmos, he said, "We know nothing about it at all. Our knowledge is but the knowledge of school children." When questioned if we would ever probe the secret, he replied, "Possibly we shall know a little more than we do now. But the real nature of things—that we shall never know, never." The Unknowable aspect of the Field is as infinite as the Field itself.

There is a pair of four variables: knower, known, process of knowing, and Field; and healer, patient, place, and Field. Each set is relevant to our connection with Self and the healing process, respectively. They both have the Field in common.

First, the knower, the known, and the process of knowing become one and blend into the Field when Samadhi and self-realization occur. This in itself constitutes extraordinary healing for that individual. The deepest healing and the patient's connection with Self are inseparable. Second, when patient (Inner Healer), healer, place, and Field all come together in a synergistic manner, there is further potential for miraculous healing.

This pair of four variables is indispensable to any patient seeking to understand the main components of healing, and the Field links them both.

Ancient wisdom has taught us that when we go beyond the hurdle of ego, we enter a more profound reality. There are various maps for gaining access to Self and, at the same time, the universal Field around us. San shamans use Num generated by the trance dance. When they travel out-of-body into the Field, they encounter the ancestral spirits and the Great Spirit as well and, in Kia, have the penetrating realization, "I feel myself again." The Yogis use austere techniques to move Kundalini energy and gain access to the cosmic Field, achieving the ultimate reality of Self (Atman) in Samadhi. The Kabbalists climb the Tree of Life to become "I am that I am." When Buddhists enter the Field, they call the experience "emptiness." As we ascend the energy hierarchy of chakras, or the Tree of Life, we encounter the unbounded potential of the Field more intensely. Depending on our culture, our conditioning, and language, distinct traditions label the appreciation differently, but the experience is universal.

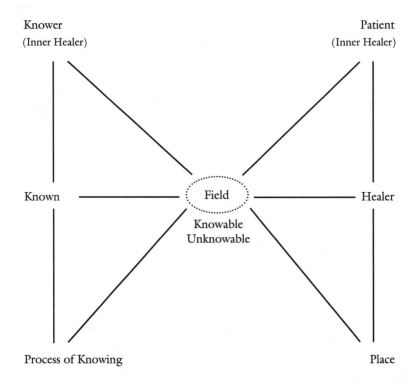

The Crucial Pair of Four Variables

We call the physical the real, and the mystical the nonreal because of our delusion. In fact, it is the other way around. The universe is all one thing, one Field of which we are a part. When we travel from the real to the nonreal and into the Field, we encounter the totality of ourselves, the material world around us, the Field, and God as one thing—unity not duality, a continuum rather than separateness. We recognize the indivisibility of all things and our total interdependency on each other and the world around us. Thich Nhat Hanh, the Buddhist monk, says we "inter are." If we practice inner techniques diligently, we may experience the possibility of an existence where we are no longer separate, detached, and disconnected.

This shift from illusion to bliss occurs if we fine-tune our energy bodies by balancing the polarities. If we are successful, this causes a change in vibration, and the energy shift that occurs in the body moves in a zigzag or spiral fashion. The higher the vibrational change, the deeper we encounter the totality of the Field.

When we are intimately connected with the Field, a certain accord occurs that has been called superfluidity by researchers of Transcendental Meditation.[3] Football players may find that everything they do flows effortlessly and flawlessly; surgeons may find themselves operating as if some greater power were controlling their actions; choirs may sing as if they had total harmonic convergence with the universe. When we are supported by the Field, magical things occur. The same is true for healing. Altered states of consciousness facilitate superfluidity.

The Field connects us all. We cannot cut down trees in the rain forest without incurring the consequences. The quantum physicist cannot observe particles without influencing their behavior, and the belief of healers in their own medicine has an effect on the potential of the patient to heal. As we will see later in this chapter, not only are the thoughts, emotions, convictions, and words of the doctor about the patient's treatment critical, but so are those of the family and friends.

We have the ability as Knowers to acknowledge the Unknowable as well as the Knowable dimensions of the Field and allow them to help us heal. This Field is encompassed by God, the Divine Presence, the Force, the Great Spirit, the Tao. There are endless possibilities in this Field, and our appreciation of its potential is limited. Statistics and prognostications for diseases should not become death sentences, since nobody has the intelligence of the real Knower. The true Knower in its purest form is the Self, within which is the Inner Healer. Like the Self, the Inner Healer is fashioned in the image of God and is supported by the immensity of the Field. The Inner Healer is divinely inspired and is responsive to messages delivered from dimensions beyond our normal state of awareness. The Inner Healer is not alone, and reinforcements are easily summoned. It is interesting that in cancer cases that have undergone spontaneous remission, a common factor found among them was a sense of "knowing" that they were going to be cured.[4]

Our Inner Healer is enabled if we intensify our internal energy, life force or Prana (breath in yoga), or Qi (pronounced Chi, in Taoist philosophy). In Hebrew, this life force is called Ruach, which also means wind, breath of life, soul, or spirit—the mysterious, unseen, and irresistible presence of the Divine Being or the spirit of God.[5] In order to enhance this vital energy and connect more intimately with the Field, we need some form of inner practice, physical or mental, such as prayer, meditation, imagery, yoga, tai chi, or the science of breath—which in yoga is called Pranayama. Imagery and visualization also help us enter the Field, and that is why they are so powerful, not only for healing, but for any pursuit; for example, gymnasts who visualize their routines before performing get better results.[6]

The Inner Healer, which heals a wound or cures a cold, resides in all of us, and becomes manifest when we are born into human form after being propagated down the Tree of Life to emerge at Malkhut. This Inner Healer is part of our life force and is linked to the universal Field around us. If we can attain supreme balance, we have the possibility of fusing with God and the Field as we experience a feeling of oneness and ecstasy. The Inner Healer, which is godlike, is expanded when we are in the space of unity consciousness. If, like the San shaman, master Kabbalist, or adept Yogi, we were able to achieve Kia, Keter, or the crown chakra, we would acquire not only the power to heal others, but the ability to help ourselves.

However, being capable of reaching evolved states of consciousness does not make us immune from or able to eliminate disease. Even enlightened beings fall prey to the ravages of illness. Nevertheless, by virtue of their ability to attain illuminated states, mystics can maintain equanimity and inner peace in the face of terrible health catastrophes and are able to transcend pain and torment. Many Buddhists transform suffering into something useful, and some welcome difficulties as challenges to test their devotion and practice. They can be healed in spirit even while disease remains in the physical body.

Even if we cannot attain these ecstatic states, any balance within the energy body will amplify the Inner Healer. Rapture, exultation, and delight help us heal. Our Inner Healer is at its most competent when it resides in joy. Love and laughter are two of the most powerful forces that augment the Inner Healer.[7,8]

The Field is nonlocal; in other words, it is not limited by space and time, and within it is the universal mind or universal consciousness. Jung would have called this the collective unconscious. Jung also described the term *synchronicity*, which occurs when an inner mental or psychic event coincides with an outer occurrence; for example, we think of a close friend whom we have not talked to in months and just then the telephone rings with that person on the line. Our interdependency and our oneness as beings are interconnected through the medium of the Field. We are all intimately related through this "mind."

Information can be transmitted telepathically via the Field in many ways. We may be close (within seeing distance), near (out of sight but in the vicinity or the general area), or far (many miles away or even in a different country or continent).

CLOSE

An example of this occurred one day when a small group of us were trekking in the mountains. I had a song on my mind and because I cannot whistle very well I kept it going inside my head. A few minutes later someone else took up the tune from my psyche and began to whistle it.

Therapeutic touch may be another example of energy crossing small distances in the Field. We have all had the feeling that someone is staring at us and when we turn around, sure enough, we see a stranger who is gazing in our direction.

NEAR

A few years ago I returned from a wilderness trek in Peru to a busy schedule of patients. One was a young athletic male whose cancerous testicle I had removed before leaving on my trek. He was scheduled to have a radical operation to remove all the lymph nodes in the back of the abdomen on my return. When I came back from my trip, he had his operation.

My schedule the next morning was due to begin early. My plan was to get up at 7 A.M., make rounds, and begin surgery at 8:30 A.M. However, I awoke at 5 A.M. with an unusual degree of clarity. In this wide-awake state I was unable to go back to sleep and lay restlessly in bed. I felt uneasy about something, but could not put my finger on it. I decided to go to the hospital to make rounds early.

It was dark when I arrived at the hospital to visit Jim. The nurse wondered what I was doing at the hospital so early and accompanied me to his bed. As we entered his room, it was obvious that Jim had stopped breathing. The nurse had seen him shortly before I arrived and everything had been fine. We began to ventilate him immediately and, because his reaction might have been due to an oversensitivity to morphine, gave him a drug called narcan, which reverses the effect of morphine. There was a dramatic response and Jim began to breathe immediately. He came to, confused and wanting to know what had happened, but none the worse for the experience.

When I left the hospital after the incident, I gave a sigh of relief and realized how different the outcome could have been if something had not awakened me that morning. I wondered if my sensitivity to messages from the Field had been increased after the past two weeks in the pristine wilderness of the Andes. Perhaps this had facilitated my relatively undeveloped shamanic powers, enabling me to tune in at some level to a possible tragedy.

FAR

People who are emotionally connected can pick up on their loved ones' anxieties, pains, and catastrophes telepathically or telesomatically (by experiencing the same symptoms in their own body), even if they are thousands of miles away. Psychics can do the same thing by interacting with the Field not only in the present, but in the past and even the future. Anyone who has witnessed the skills of a psychic or trance channel knows this to be true. These messages can be extremely useful if we are able to receive and read them.

When my son Terry and I were nearly shot on the Botswana border, my other son Paul was hundreds of miles away in the Okavango swamps. At the same time we were experiencing our own panic, Paul had a severe anxiety attack and told his friend that something grave had happened to us. Anxiety attacks are entirely out of character for Paul.

Unfortunately, to the uninitiated Westerner such as myself, a directive given is often easily ignored. It might appear in a dream, as in my experience in Manu before I fractured my wrist, in the waking state as a gut feeling, or as a sensation that something is not quite right. A psychic healer's or shaman's ability to read signals from the Field is much more developed, but there is no reason why we cannot also develop this capacity, given confidence and practice.

If information can be picked up at a distance, it can also be transmitted in the opposite direction. Research has shown that images can be transferred from one person to another acting as the receiver in a remote area. The images are sometimes distorted, but the context is maintained even if the exact symbol is less clear.[9,10]

I was convinced of this during an experiment a group of us conducted in Machu Picchu, Peru, with shaman Don Eduardo Calderon. Half the group had hiked to the Temple of the Moon on Waynu Picchu, a peak adjacent to these ancient ruins. The other half remained in the ruins themselves and were performing a healing ceremony and meditation with Eduardo. Those of us in the cave at the Temple of the Moon had been asked to project an image to Eduardo that he would pick up while meditating in the ruins. Later, we would confirm how accurate his Field antenna had been. We chose the sign on a dollar bill—a circle with a pyramid inside. When we later conferred with Eduardo, he said he had received an image of a circular opening resembling the mouth of a cave, and in it was a triangle.

What if two or more individuals are involved and there is a coherence of attention projected into the Field? Maharishi Mahesh Yogi has described the Maharishi effect in association with Transcendental Meditation. The effect states that the more the number of meditators in a particular city or place, the more positive the benefits. This can be documented as a decrease in the crime rate, as well as other beneficial changes. The group consciousness or mind coherence set up by the meditators has a positive result on everyone else in the vicinity of this mini-field, and even beyond. The Maharishi International University has documented many examples of this. Maharishi is only confirming what Eastern mysticism has held for millennia: consciousness extends beyond the individual and is nonlocal in its effects on the Field.

The effects of this type of coherence can also be measured in a device as mechanical as an electronic random number generator (RNG), with the combined attention being something as impersonal as millions of people watching a sports event on TV.[11] The focus of these viewers affects the way an RNG selects its sequence of numbers. If we extend this principle to healing, such remote influences can be extremely important. The nonlocal effect of coherent awareness is likely to be even more powerful when a meditative state is used and there is a specific focus or goal in mind (as opposed to passively watching a TV event). If the intention is to heal a patient, this could constitute powerful medicine.

Coherence of group consciousness may be the reason why prayer from a distance can favorably affect a recipient. Furthermore, cancer support groups or medical teams working together on medical dilemmas may be more effective by virtue of their attention and intention even when not in direct contact with the group or the patient. Since each healer communicates with the Field, the Inner Healer of the patient is able to glean support from a remote but mutually cohesive force.

When I worked at Stanford Medical Center, I was always struck by the fact that there was a certain synergy that seemed to go beyond the particular treatment dispensed. This may have been a result of the combined concentration given to the challenge by the medical team in, and even beyond, the walls of the institution. The team frequently took the patient's problem home with them, thereby maintaining a connection with the patient via the Field. This non-local effect may explain the extraordinary results achieved by big referral centers that can be difficult to emulate in the private practice setting where fewer caregivers are involved.

Most of us can accept that grace from God may create miracles of healing nonlocally through the Field, but can ordinary mortals achieve similar benefits by sending healing energy to patients? Psychic healers and shamans are adamant that this can be done from close, near, or far. There is scientific evidence for an effect that works through the Field. Proof that messages and healing can be transmitted via the Field is available from many sources.[12,13]

Prayer has been shown to have beneficial effects on the sick. When patients know they are being prayed for, improvements in health could be explained as due to the placebo response. However, when patients are unaware prayers are being delivered, we can safely assume that the placebo effect is not involved.

Patients who were prayed for while recovering from massive heart attacks in intensive care units were found to do better than a comparable control group who did not receive prayers. Those who were prayed for did not know prayers were being sent by people unknown to them from a distance. The group that was prayed for had fewer complications, required less pain medicine, and were discharged from the unit sooner.[14]

Larry Dossey[15] suggests that nondirected prayer may be more effective than directed prayer. Directed prayer assumes that healing will unfold in a specific way outlined by the prayer, whereas nondirected prayer implies "Thy will be done."

To a true believer, it seems logical that nondirected prayer would be more potent, since God knows exactly what is required and we may only get in the way by trying to program the result. Directing details to God of what should happen seems somewhat presumptuous. Certainly, as laymen, and even as physicians, we may have the wrong idea of what is required, and the Field may know best. We may get in the way by trying to influence the outcome. The idea that nondirected prayer works best may, however, be a very personal matter. The philosopher Martin Buber said, "All men have access to God but each man has a different access." Someone who is religious, inwardly directed, and God fearing may be more effective with a nondirected approach, whereas someone who is goal and externally oriented may do better with a directed method. Healing is such a mystery; we can only hope that the Field and the Divine Spirit will get the general idea and assist with the process, no matter how clumsy we are with our prayers.

Physician Deepak Chopra has confirmed the spiritual principle that releasing our desires into the cosmos is more effective if we are in a meditative state.[16] He emphasizes setting ego aside, being unattached to the outcome, and allowing the universe (Field) to handle the details. This resembles an endorsement for nondirected prayer. Since the Field is part of God's manifestation, it seems logical that the best way to approach it is by surpassing ego and leaving desirous attachment behind.

Fred Sicher recently published an article in the Western Journal of Medicine after five years of research by a team at California Pacific Medical Center involving AIDS patients. The patients comprised a control group and a treatment group; they were carefully matched for severity of disease. The two groups were blinded so neither knew who was getting treated, thus eliminating the possibility of a placebo response. Those who were treated received psychic healing from afar from an experienced group of healers over a period of two months. There was a 40 percent mortality in the control group and none in the treatment arm. The treatment group did significantly better than the control group on numerous parameters (AIDS-defining diseases, overall illness severity, number of hospitalizations, length of hospital stay when admitted, severity of depression, anger, anxiety, and overall vigor). This effect has now earned recognition from the National Institute of Health who have termed it "distant mental influence on biological systems."[17]

Most alternative healers and psychics who give healing and paranormal assistance agree that healing can be done from a distance; the subject does not have to be present or aware of the process for it to work. While a healer can heal someone far away, a sorcerer can create disease and even death from a distance with a hex. White or black magic has been known for millennia, but is only now being validated by science. Although it sounds implausible to the Western mind, cultures in Africa, South America, and elsewhere have no trouble accepting it. Prayer or negative imagery can have both beneficial or adverse effects. These effects are nonlocal, and we can assume they work through the Field. The Field, therefore, appears impartial to bad morals or evil motivation from the perpetrator. Voodoo, however, is done with direct knowledge of the victim, and this *nocebo* effect (opposite of placebo in that it creates harm rather than healing) is distinctly local in nature. The damaging power of nocebo is susceptible to the belief system of the victim.

Physician Larry Dossey, in his thought-provoking book *Healing Words*,[18] gives an excellent review of the relevant literature on this subject. He also discusses the death prayer of the kahuna shamans in Hawaii. This was administered in times past to those who were deserving of severe punishment. It was felt to work

through the mechanism of guilt and an inner realization by vic-
tims that they deserved to die. When the verdict and sentence
were given, they were dispensed from afar without the knowledge
of the guilty party. In other words, the effect was not local or
voodoo related. The combination of this death wish from the
outside and the guilt from within were felt to be as certain as any
death decree.

In any situation, guilt has a noxious effect, not only on our
soul, but also on the healing process. The soul, the Inner Healer,
and healing are inseparable. Ancient wisdom reminds us that we
cannot have a positive effect on our spiritual progress if we have a
poor image of our self-worth. Guilt can inhibit attempts to align
with our higher Self. Connection with Self is a vital part of getting well. All religions have strict ethical and moral codes to help
us link with our Divine essence because it was realized that guilt
arising from misconduct will hamper our spiritual progress (as it
will hamper the course of healing).

Guilt comes from our cultural and religious conditioning, and
sometimes may have no ethical foundation. We all feel guilty for
many different reasons. In some situations, we may impose a
kahuna-style curse on ourselves. Sexual guilt, especially, seems to
create an additional guilt burden because it is so emotionally
charged. Some patients may feel they deserve to be sick and/or
they are not entitled to get well.

The Field does not seem to discriminate between good and
bad or right and wrong because it also honors the evil intentions
of black magic. Whether prayers for healing are more effective
than evil imagery is unknown. Whether dark visualizations are
stronger than light is unclear. History, however, tells us that light
will eventually prevail over dark. Hitler was a specialist in the dark
forces of the occult. Maybe good triumphs in the end because
even the soul of the most heinous human knows right from
wrong, and the guilt that is imprinted there may adversely affect
the life force, causing good to win out in the end. The law of
karma (of cause and effect) states that at the soul level no one

gets away with harmful intentions and this is why we are born again and again. We come back to make amends so we can align our higher selves to the Divine.

To many of us, especially with Judeo-Christian backgrounds, karma may appear to be a law of life imposed from the outside by God. If we live unskillfully, God sees to it that we come back again to rectify our behavior. However, it seems more plausible that karma is a default inherent in the nature of the soul itself. Karma may occur from within rather than from without. We create our own reality, and if we create an existence that is malevolent, we will eventually come to endure the consequences. The soul imposes its own sentence on itself. The kahunas may have realized something very profound about the repercussions of guilt. A hex placed on a guilty party may be especially potent. Possibly the karmic "receptor" of the soul becomes hypersensitive where guilt abounds. Guilt may immobilize the life force and the Inner Healer. We must remind ourselves that guilt has no place in the healing mechanism.

If doctors have an appreciation of their own weaknesses, they may be better able to understand their patients' dilemmas. Healers need to recognize their patient's anguish and lack of equilibrium, and know that but for a twist of fate, they may have been in a similar predicament. With more compassion and empathy, and by realizing the nature of the Field, healers can recognize their ability to facilitate or aggravate the patient's Inner Healer not only by their deeds, words, and body language, but also by their wishes and thoughts. The positive desires and prayers of the physician are just as important as the affirmations and visualizations of the patient in facilitating the healing process.

NOTES

1. Talbot, Michael. *The Holographic Universe.* New York: Harper Perennial, 1991.

2. Ring, Kenneth. *Life at Death.* New York: Quill, 1980.

3. Chopra, Deepak, M.D. *Perfect Health.* New York: Harmony Books, 1991.

4. Siegel, Bernie. *Love, Medicine and Miracles: Lessons Learned from a Surgeon's Experience with Exceptional Patients.* New York: Harper Row, 1990.

5. *Pentateuch and Haftorahs*, from Genesis, Edited by Dr. J. H. Hertz. London: Soncino Press, 1981.

6. Garfield, Charles. *Peak Performance: Mental Training Techniques of the World's Greatest Athletes.* New York: Warner Books, 1984.

7. Cousins, Norman. *Anatomy of an Illness.* New York: Norton, 1995.

8. Ornish, Dean. *Love and Survival.* New York: Harper Collins, 1998.

9. Dossey, Larry, M.D. *Healing Words.* San Francisco: Harper Collins, 1994.

10. Talbot, *The Holographic Universe.*

11. Radin, Dean. "Moving Mind. Moving Matter." (extract from The Conscious Universe) *Noetic Sciences Review*, no. 46. Summer 1998.

12. Dossey, *Healing Words.*

13. Talbot, *The Holographic Universe.*

14. "Positive Therapeutic Effects of Intercessory Prayer in a Coronary Care Unit Population." *Southern Medical Journal*, vol. 81, no. 7. July 1988: 826–829.

15. Dossey, *Healing Words.*

16. Talbot, *The Holographic Universe.*

17. Targ, Elisabeth. "Distant Healing." *Noetic Sciences Review*, no. 49. August–November 1999: 24.

18. Dossey, *Healing Words.*

THE TREE OF HEALTH

A Tree of Health is another model that helps us juggle and prevail over the opposites. Thoughts lead to words, and words can indeed "call" positive or negative events into existence.

The Tree of Life discussed in chapter 6 is intimately involved with all four variables of healing. For the patient, it is a pathway to the higher Self, and also a way to better health. For the healer, it is a model to achieve balance and more effective healing. The Field is the source of multiple healing possibilities for patient and healer, and we all yearn for a hallowed sanctuary, or a metaphoric Eden, where we can find inner peace.

The central trunk of the Tree embraces the concepts of *Will*, *Balance*, and *Grace*. Will holds the balance, or maintains the equilibrium of the Tree of Life. Grace can enter at any time, especially at the level of Daat on the Tree. Healing occurs through these three essential properties on the central limb of the Tree.

Grace is from God and becomes manifest in the power of our Inner Healer to eliminate disease. Grace can be assisted by the efforts and prayers of the patient, the

129

healer, and anyone else. Many psychic healers say that they are not doing the healing, but rather channeling a power from a higher source. They may be connecting the Inner Healer of the patient with the Divine force inherent in the Field. Will, determination, or resolution come from the desire of the patient to be well. Balance occurs by attending to the various polarities on the Tree of Life, and requires some form of receptive or inner practice. When the patient is centered in the middle of the Tree of Life, they have greater access to the Field.

We have seen how some South American shamans use a mesa, a table-like altar, as a tool for healing. Implicit in the mesa is the idea of balance or equilibrium. The dark, evil, or negative facets that create illness are on the left-hand side and the light, positive or healing attributes are on the right. The shaman heals by staying in the center of the mesa and balancing these opposites.

It occurred to me that it might be useful if I could devise a similar model of healing that is concordant not only with the idea of the mesa, but also with the principles of the Tree of Life. In this way, I hoped, I might come closer to a true understanding of what the complexities of healing are all about. I have called this model a Tree of Health. A Tree of Health involves three of the four healing factors—healer, patient, and Field. By staying in the center of the Tree of Health, patients and their physicians can attain balance, healing, and self-restoration. In the discussion that follows, key words will be capitalized and italicized for emphasis.

The polarities of the Tree of Health that will be developed are:

Left: Restrains, Contracts, and Inhibits through Hopelessness, Resignation, Fear, Guilt, Denial, Ignorance, Lack of Choice, and Inaction.

Right: Expands, Facilitates, and Strengthens through Hope or Trust, Belief or Faith, Surrender, Love, Courage, Truth, Knowledge, Receptivity, Choice, and Right Action.

Center: Balance and Equilibrium result in inner peace and harmony and support the Inner Healer. Through the Center, the patient's Life Force communicates with the Field. Inner practices facilitate this contact and enhance the Life Force (Prana, Qi, Ruach). Calling our wish to be healed creates Intention, which with balance, leads to healing. Grace may enter at any time and its ultimate expression is spontaneous healing. When we find our center or we center ourselves, we are balanced in the core of a Tree of Health.

Left	Center	Right
Inhibits	Will/Balance (Inner Practices)	Expands
Hopelessness		Hope/Trust Faith/Belief
	Life Force	
Resignation		Surrender Receptivity
Fear		Love
Guilt	Will	Courage
Denial	Calling or Naming Creating and Intention Formulating	Truth
Ignorance		Knowledge
Lack of Choice		Choice
Inaction	Grace	Right Action

The Tree of Health

Each patient's connection with his or her Inner Healer via the Field is unique. Therefore, different aspects of the Tree of Health may work for some but not for others. This will depend on sex, genetics, culture, religion, education, and conditioning.

There are two essential qualities for healing to occur at the deepest level: Belief and hope. Belief or faith, and hope or trust support the will to be well.

BELIEF AND HOPE

When the first white settlers in South Africa encountered the San people, they reported that if perfectly healthy San were imprisoned, they would die quickly and inexplicably in their cells. Since the San live so much in the present moment, the absence of any *Hope* of being freed destroyed the will to live and dissipated the life force. We should never underestimate the significance of hope on the life force.

Belief and hope boost the effectiveness of the Inner Healer— the "placebo response." The healer who is aware of the power of belief on the Inner Healer of the patient can put this placebo effect to good use. The stronger the belief that the patient has in the healer, the more the trust and greater the empathy, the more profound the influence of placebo. Whereas placebo is almost a bad word to the Western doctor, it goes to the core of healing, which is the relationship between the physician, the therapy, and the Inner Healer of the patient. Some doctors exude a sense of unruffled calm, certainty, trust, composure, and confidence that augments the placebo effect.

Activation of the Inner Healer occurs within the belief system of the patient. At one level or another, the healer is also treating the patient's own specific consciousness and conviction. Ultimately, this will translate into better alignment of the patient's energy body. Most Western physicians do not have the training or the time to deal with illness in this way. Nevertheless, they need to pay attention to it in order to more effectively help their patients. If healers disturb the belief system of the patient by the imposition of their own belief, they will compromise the magical ability of the system to work. Faith or belief in the healer is critical, and there must be a consistency between the patient's notion of healing and the doctor's approach. A Westerner may be satisfied with a written prescription and explanation as to how the medication is going to work; a San patient would trust a hands-on approach combined with some sweat from a San dancer in a posttrance state.

Physicians are well aware of the fact that experimental trials on new drugs are often successful when they are first introduced. Hope may have a lot to do with this. When the drugs are studied later by other groups, the success rate seems to drop off. The patient's hope and belief that a new therapy can cure, and the enthusiasm of the investigating team that it will work can lead to spectacular results. The patient has no prior knowledge that this treatment may not be effective and neither do the physicians. Subsequent trials on the new drug may be less successful because the examining team may be skeptical about the findings and the optimistic reports. This dubious attitude may supervene and negate the initial impact of hope. If physicians dispense treatments they do not believe in, this weakens the placebo effect by contracting the Field of possibilities.

When the oncologist tells the patient that there is a 50 percent chance that the drug or chemotherapy might not work, the power of hope has been divided in half. For the treatment to work optimally, the patient *and* the physician must believe in, and be hopeful about, its effectiveness. Due to the fact that the relationship between patient and physician is not something that can be quantified, we may never be able to truly measure the result of a treatment because placebo or belief cannot be entirely extracted and isolated.

What exactly is the *Doctor-Patient Relationship?* This is a special alliance formed, not only between the patient and the doctor, but also between the Inner Healer of the patient and all the physician has to offer. Certain physicians are more influential than others, even when the same treatment is administered. This occurs because of a special bond of belief, hope, and trust that arises between patient and doctor. A lack of trust or belief in the physician could be harmful, and even toxic, to the patient's health. No patient should be forced to put up with an interaction that creates disharmony. The deeper effects of this alliance needs to be appreciated fully during this era of "managed care" in the United States. Managed-care insurance companies think that any "Doc in a box" form of supermarket care will do, and that an interpersonal relationship between patient and healer is of little consequence. For the Inner Healer to be most proficient, the patient has to make a special association with their physician, and this requires an active *Choice* of who is the best healer for the task. Patients who, for financial or other reasons, have access to a fixed panel of doctors with few options, may have their own special needs compromised. This may not matter for the average medical problem, but can become vital when managing difficult health challenges.

The implications of the word "provider" in the phrase "health care provider" has succeeded in demolishing the doctor-patient relationship, which has been crucial to healing for eons. Synonyms given by a thesaurus for the word "provider," include: pimp, panderer, runner, agent, hustler, supplier, purveyor, and procurer. This kind of loose and insulting labeling of physicians goes to the heart of undermining the essence of healing itself. Most of us need the vital healing energy a compassionate healer can give us to help trigger our Inner Healer.

Additional stimulation of the Inner Healer can come from joy, prayer, support, love, or grace, but we should never underestimate the importance of the doctor-patient relationship, which is vital to the placebo response.

Hope, of course, is a serious undertaking because it may require the hard work that will demands of it. Not everyone is committed to working hard to achieve the balance required for healing, achieving, or maintaining optimal health. A friend of mine is fond of saying, "Ever since I gave up hope, I feel much better!" There is comfort in resignation. We can let go, believe there is nothing more to be done, and let nature take its course. In its most extreme form, this may take the form of a death request. There are times when this approach is entirely appropriate, but there are others when it is not.

RESIGNATION VERSUS SURRENDER

Resignation, withdrawal, and abandoning hope may be a manifestation of indifference or apathy, laziness or passivity, and desperation or hopelessness, all of which lead to inaction. Fear may also play a part.

Hopelessness and resignation are not the same as *Surrender*. Surrender implies letting go and allowing a higher force to take over; it is the ultimate expression of unconditional hope and belief —a job-like attitude—that trusts that whatever arises is for the best. The patient feels gratitude and acceptance and is content to just be. Eastern philosophies affirm the power of not doing, of not grasping, of going with the flow, of being in the Tao. The Buddhist appreciation of the emptiness that arises from not grasping requires a different kind of motivation and sustained dedication that is difficult to attain. By going into the silence of not grasping, we communicate more directly with the Field. Surrender connects us to the Field, while resignation and hopelessness separate us from it. Surrender is fearless and does not exclude the use of medical attention. Resignation implies desperation or depression, which is known to suppress the immune system.

Accepting one's disease as part of oneself may be considered a form of surrender. By not recognizing it as "other" or "bad," no duality is created and it may be easier to attain the equanimity necessary for healing or cure. This may be a helpful way of coping with the truth of the diagnosis. Visualizations that project the disease as a hideous enemy or ogre may be unsuitable for certain individuals; they may create fear and its associated emotions that inhibit the immune system. Furthermore, with a friendlier attitude to the challenge, less effort is required to learn the lessons the illness provides. The disease may even appear to be a gift which has lead to an essential transformational change. The metamorphosis may not have happened without it. The patient becomes open and flexible rather than rigid, aggressive, and confrontational about their predicament. Surrender leads to a greater *Receptivity* to the available options, which can be an advantage.

Passive resignation with an underlying hopelessness is not the same as the active and joyous acceptance of surrender. Surrender arises from a deep connection with the Field, an acknowledgment of a higher power working through it, and an appreciation of the life force and the strength of the Inner Healer. This comes from a strong desire to be well and an understanding that whatever may happen, the disease can be regarded as a teacher from which gifts and benefits come, even if a cure does not result. Our most powerful inner experiences often occur in the space of severe pain and suffering, and from these flow our most heartfelt prayers. This gift is sometimes proportional to the degree of misery inflicted. For many of us, it is only through a dark night of the soul that we acquire the grail, and the illness may assume the archetype of a hero's journey. We could not have attained the blessing any other way. Surrender can promote healing, whereas the despondency and sorrow associated with resignation inhibits the Inner Healer and the immune system. All healers have seen special people with AIDS, cancer, and other diseases where the condition has resulted in a greater inner peace and wholeness and an incomparable zest for life—surrender rather than resignation. This profound form of spirituality needs to arise from within in order to be authentic. It cannot be contrived or superficially stated.

Surrender usually invokes a certain humility and subordination of the ego. Therefore, the boon that arises from surrender is affiliation with the higher Self. Yoga and Buddhism teach that desirous attachment (which is part of ego) is one of the greatest obstacles on the enlightenment path. When we reach Keter, or the crown chakra, we experience the Divine within and without, and we detach from the goal of health, or anything else for that matter. We just are; we attain pure being. If we lose the fear or the attachment we have to being cured, we may be healed and possibly even cured.

FEAR

There are two basic emotions: *Love* and *Fear*. Love is always good for healing. Fear is usually bad. *Courage* counteracts fear and, although bravery is usually part of one's makeup, it can be nurtured and developed. As discussed above, fear is also part of resignation and hopelessness.

Disease creates fear, with associated anxiety, alienation, and isolation. Fear and stress elicit a response called the fight-or-flight reaction from the autonomic nervous system, which results from a cognitive appraisal of a threat. In the case of disease, this may be a threat to life, limb, organ, or function. The possibility that life may be short-lived or never the same again leads to a range of harmful emotions related to fear. This elicits a response from the adrenal gland, which pours out the hormones necessary for a fight or flight reaction. The reaction is entirely appropriate if one is being chased by a bear, but is unhealthy on a chronic basis; it is tailored to get us out of a short-term emergency predicament. If the reaction persists, too much adrenaline overloads the cardiovascular system, and excess cortisone taxes and exhausts the immune system, which may even promote diabetes. Morbid fear can completely overwhelm the Inner Healer.

GUILT

Guilt can create shame, humiliation, or mortification—pernicious forces not only in healing, but in many circumstances. According to the West African shaman Malidoma Some:

> *Shame (guilt) is seen in Dagara culture as a collapsing emotional force that paralyzes the Self and therefore, like grief,*

should only be experienced in a sacred ceremonial context . . . .
Shame compresses the psyche dangerously . . . one experiences
crippling rejection and ostracism as one's self-esteem is almost
exterminated . . . this is comparable to death.[1]

Dread of the consequences of failure causes ineffectiveness, help-lessness, and a feeling of worthlessness that generates *Guilt*. Guilt may also be aggravated by a New Age misconception that not only has the patient caused the illness, but they have the ability to correct it as well. When a cure does not occur, this may lead to a sense of defeat, resignation, and guilt, which debilitate the Inner Healer. The physician can significantly aggravate the situation by giving a gloomy or hopeless prognosis, and the alternative healer can increase guilt by accusing the patient of bringing on the disease or not wanting to get well.

DENIAL

Denial may be a subconscious manifestation of fear. For some, denial can be a powerful coping mechanism. This seems a contradiction, since denial would appear to be self-defeating when it comes to health. In the short-term, however, denial may help the patient get over the terror of a medical crisis. The patient's subconscious may know that true knowledge of the predicament may be too much to handle at that critical time. Denial may be good in these special circumstances, but not when it prevents the person from going to the hospital in the first instance. A friend of mine with heart disease had a fatal attack one day while mowing the lawn. He chose to deny and ignore the chest pain and kept mowing until it was too late. Resignation may have played some part in this, since he was lonely and seemed tired of life. His choice to continue mowing may have been a subtle form of suicide. The occasional patient with advanced cancer will deny the diagnosis and believe unquestionably that they will become well. These exceptional patients sometimes remain in remission or are even cured.

IGNORANCE

Ignorance can be like denial, useful in certain predicaments but probably not in the long-term. When I trained in the American system, I realized that a different psychological approach was used in each country. The South African physicians hardly ever told their patients the diagnosis, and many patients were unaware of the fact they had cancer. In the United States, almost everyone was told their diagnosis; nevertheless, the results in the two systems appeared the same. Superficially, it would seem that ignorance of the condition might cause less fear and a longer survival. This was not a case of denial, but of ignorance. However, every patient probably knew at a subconscious level that they had cancer, and this may have dictated the outcome. If you added to this the physician's and the families' silent knowledge of the problem, and the local and nonlocal projection of this awareness onto the patient, it was hardly surprising that the outcome was equivalent, whether the patient was told or not. In fact, ignorance plus a vivid imagination could have aggravated fear, and the patient may have believed they had a much graver outlook than was so.

TRUTH

Without the *Truth* about the nature of the disease, the patient has no idea of the extent of the challenge. There is something especially liberating about the truth. The most important thing about illness may well be the lessons it brings about our attitudes and our lifestyle. Without knowledge of the truth, it is unlikely we will learn the teaching—even if we are cured we may have to confront our deficiencies at a later date.

Truth and the Diagnosis: Truth implies a correct diagnosis is made so the remedy can match the condition. Just knowing the diagnosis can be reassuring, and is therapy in itself. The Inner Healer can then come to grips with the challenge and do its job. Confusion as to the diagnosis and treatment can increase fear and inhibit the Inner Healer. Many patients are optimistic when they know their diagnosis—they can do something tangible to treat the problem. Knowing the condition is not serious (for instance, that stress can cause pain in an organ from muscle tension), can be treatment in itself. If a patient understands that pain can lead to a vicious cycle of more stress, more tension in the smooth muscle, and more pain, knowledge of this dynamic alone can break the pain cycle—the common complaint of the irritable bowel syndrome is a good example.

I am reminded of a patient who was losing a lot of blood every month from very heavy periods due to a large fibroid tumor in her uterus. Initially, she saw an internist who correctly diagnosed the problem, prescribed iron, and suggested a hysterectomy if the symptoms persisted. She reacted adversely to the iron supplements, became disenchanted with the Western approach, and saw a Chinese doctor who diagnosed liver imbalance. The anemia became worse over time, and the Chinese herbs were clearly ineffective. Following this, other alternative methods were employed. Ultimately, after collapsing one day from profound anemia, she received a blood transfusion, her uterus was removed, and she regained her normal state of health. For treatment to be effective, the diagnosis must be true, or correct. Good intentions and "aligning the body's meridians" may be insufficient.

Truth and Denial: Denial may lead to a deluded sense of what is appropriate action, resulting in failure. The patient has to be realistic about the undertaking, or there will be a mismatch between the energy required for healing and the effort expended for the task. Denial may help us feel better temporarily, but in the long-term, truth is a more powerful agent. Denial may be good palliation, but truth may be more curative. Truth is the antidote to denial and ignorance.

Truth and Fear—The Prognosis: Physicians, with their scientific training, feel obligated to tell patients the truth. They may quote statistics, such as, "You only have six months to live because you have stage X and grade Y of disease Z." This can be a powerful negative visualization, and even a type of voodoo curse or hex. Whereas the prognosis given by the oncologist may be administered without intent to do harm, it can be an evil spell with a prophecy of doom which may become self-fulfilling. Only exceptional patients can rise above this prediction and determine their own destiny with disease.

For some patients it may even be preferable to withhold the diagnosis because of their unique conditioning, culture, or education. Knowledge of such a calamity might completely immobilize them with horror and trepidation. For this reason, withholding diagnoses is a common practice outside of the United States. I remember being told during my training by one of my professors in South Africa that we should never tell a patient that they had cancer unless they had some critical financial decisions to make. Unfortunately, this physician had a patient commit suicide when he learned his diagnosis.

I try not to give my patient's statistics about their possible outcome. In the end, it is arrogant to believe that in our limited capacity as healers we know the truth about the patient, the Inner Healer, the Field, and God, as well as the countless other factors that cannot be measured.

Truth and Physician Fear: American physicians are frequently motivated to tell the whole truth, and nothing but the truth because of their own fear. This is a result of the litigious nature of our society. There always seems to be a phantom attorney sitting on the patient's bed dictating the doctor's decisions. No medic wants to be sued for lack of full disclosure. "Informed consent" before invasive procedures requires listing all conceivable complications related to diagnosis and therapy. This custom creates unnecessary fear and anxiety. The truth, or informed consent prior to medical procedures, can be delivered in an informative, supportive, nurturing manner with due regard for the patient's sensitivities. There are different ways of telling the truth, and delivery of the message does not have to be detached, rough-handed, or cruel. Giving enough facts to inform but not terrify the patient is a vital clinical skill. The physician's fear of the legal system should not be transmuted into terror for the patient.

The raw truth may elicit fear, which may be a negative factor in healing, but a balanced and hopeful look at the truth can be a grand transformational tool that induces the changes required for better health. A patient who is knowledgeable about their condition without being debilitated by the fear of its consequences can rise to the challenge and gain a sense of command. Knowledge of one's predicament can give a sense of control and lessen fear. Ignorance is not necessarily bliss; being well-versed and taking charge gives us a feeling of direction, which counteracts fear and all its adverse ramifications.

There has been an overemphasis on words in this chapter, but words help strike at the core of disease. If we look at Genesis, we see that "in the beginning was the word," and that God "called" or "named" the entire universe into being. We must not underestimate the power of the spoken word, since it was God's word that called matter into existence.

In Kabbalah, there are four separate but interconnected Trees of Life representing the four distinct phases of creation of the universe and of man. The first is Emanation (calling or naming); the second is the Tree of Creation; the third is Formation; and the fourth tree is Making. For instance, at first there was the concept of Adam (or calling or naming), followed by the creation of the design of Adam (or the plan or the *Intention*). This led to Adam's formation, until he was made in human form in the Garden of Eden. In fact, anything that becomes manifest, wellness included, also goes through these distinct four phases.

First we name or call it something, and then we create the plan, the scheme, or the intention. The formation process follows and, ultimately, the final product is made. Kabbalah states that God can create something out of nothing. Humans, on the other hand, only have the ability to produce things out of something already existing. We should recognize that there are four potential phases in the creation of health and, for the sake of helping our Inner Healer, we should give each stage its due attention. Since our Inner Healer is fashioned in the image of God, it knows the alchemy required to create health out of disease.

We can call or name wellness into being, and then create a plan, or an intention, to be well. Our will, or resolution, gets behind that intention. Intention is followed by formulation and, finally, *Action,* or doing what is appropriate for the challenge at hand. Action is phase four, which is the making of health.

Without the balance implicit in the various polarities of the Tree of Life and a Tree of Health, our resolution, or will, can lead us astray. Will has to be realistic and tailored to the task at hand. This is where the knowledge of the medical profession can be extremely useful.

Calling or naming, followed by intention that is intelligent, creates action that is appropriate rather than misdirected. For action to be most effective, active choice and *Participation* of the patient are required. True or right action requires that the patient has a say in the decision. Passive patients who allow the health team to make all the decisions, regardless of how they feel about the consequences, are disabled patients—the power of will is at least partly deactivated, and balance is disturbed. On the other hand, there are passive patients who have made a choice to have complete hope and faith in the medical team, and allow them to do whatever is deemed fit. This can be part of the surrender approach and, in this way, intention and correct action occur automatically if the competence of the medical effort matches the confidence granted it.

Belief and hope rather than hopelessness; surrender rather than resignation; love and courage rather than fear; truth rather than denial; knowledge and receptivity rather than ignorance; choice rather than lack of choice; action rather than inaction—all of these together with will and balance are a powerful combination and, when strengthened by grace, can be a formidable remedy for healing or cure. It behooves all healers to be sure this prescription is taken in generous amounts.

A Tree of Health is another model that helps us juggle and prevail over the opposites. Thoughts lead to words, and words can indeed "call" positive or negative events into existence. Once we put our thoughts into words, we have begun the process of emanation. It is difficult to curb negative thoughts unless we refine our minds with some sort of meditative practice. However, we should stop short of translating thoughts into words. We strengthen or weaken our equanimity depending on how we describe, depict, emphasize, accentuate, highlight, articulate, elaborate, regard, detail, and even joke about our inner being and health. When we complain, bewail, moan, grumble, protest, remonstrate, itemize, and verbalize negatively, we may do ourselves harm. Since everything began with the word, we have to be careful with thoughts that lead to pessimistic speech. We can guard our reflections by paying attention to how we contemplate, mirror, picture, muse, survey, observe, regard, brood, weigh, consider, speculate, ponder, and plan. If we dwell on those meanings on the right side of the Tree of Health, we align with health. If we stress the dark aspects on the left, we do the opposite. We should strengthen and facilitate the positive conversation and beware of delving into negative dialogue. If we stay centered, the greatest possibility for wholeness and health may manifest. A Tree of Health helps us remember the essential factors that influence the Inner Healer, and reinforces the concept of polarity balance that is the key to all healing.

NOTES

1. Some, Malidoma Patrice. *The Healing Wisdom of Africa*. New York: Penguin Putnam, Inc., 1998.

HEALING OUTCOMES

A state of inner peace is not reliant on a healthy body. Depending on our skill with transpersonal development, we can attain blissful states of being and be plagued with disease at the same time.

Depending on the interaction between the Inner Healer of the patient, the healer, the Field, and sometimes the power of place, the following outcomes of disease can occur: spontaneous remission, a balance between patient and disease, relapse, fulminating progression and death, and being healed but not cured.

SPONTANEOUS REMISSION

The ultimate expression of the competence of the Inner Healer can be seen in patients with incurable conditions who undergo spontaneous remission. When the four forces of Inner Healer, physician, Field, and place are in complete alignment, spontaneous remission is more likely occur. Spontaneous remission is a little like seeing water flowing uphill—a disease, which is hopeless by Western medical standards, disappears.

The mechanism for this marvel may be total vibrational realignment of the body's energy system. Most diseases probably start at a subatomic level in the cells after the disorder begins in the energy body. For spontaneous healing to occur, the malady must be corrected at a subatomic level as well. The core belief of balance helps us access our inner being, or higher Self, which is directly connected to the Inner Healer. When we are aligned with the higher Self at Keter, or the crown chakra, and the Kundalini or Num has risen up the spine, our energy body is in balance. For this to happen, we must open up the heart chakra to love, forgiveness, compassion, and empathy, both for ourselves and for others. In the Kabbalistic model, we need to move the energy to Tiferet, the heart of the Tree, and above. This receptivity is a more feminine skill. Children are familiar with the power of a mother's love in facilitating the Inner Healer when they are ill.

The masculine force, on the other hand, is associated more with intellect and ego, which is implemented by the third chakra, or Yesod. These give us the drive to heal and help us to cognitively find balance. Both polarities are essential, but Western custom overemphasizes the latter.

The helical structure of the DNA is represented in the chakra system and in the symbol of the caduceus. There are two spirals in each complex, and these exemplify the polarities, feminine and masculine, yin and yang, dark and light, contraction and expansion, moon and sun, left and right sides of the Tree of Life. They also epitomize the dichotomy between science and mysticism, between modern medicine and the healing magic of faith and hope. We need both polarities and both spirals to heal.

Especially when it comes to cancer and AIDS, healing must occur at the level of DNA in the cell, at the level of the blueprint of life itself. The spirals seen in the chakra system, the DNA helix, and the caduceus can be extrapolated to every living thing in the cosmos. As is the microcosm, so is the macrocosm. To heal, the Kundalini or Num must align the energy at the level of each atom in the DNA and in the cell. Ayahuasca shamans are very familiar with the archetypal image of the helix in their healing ceremonies, and this has profound symbolic significance to the mechanisms of how we heal.[1] Vibrational energy moves up the sun and moon channels and presumably up the DNA helix in a zigzag, lightning, or spiral manner endowed by the shape of this pathway. This energy that vibrates in a spiral is not only within us, but is also universal and part of the Field. This emphasizes the fact that the Field only appears to lie outside of us. In actuality, we are all part of one vibrational, cosmic Field or the hologram of the universe.[2]

Alignment of the energy coursing through our nadis does not have to be as dramatic as a full-blown Kundalini experience. Any inner discipline that balances the opposite masculine yang polarity, or purely cognitive aspect of allopathic medical science, will allow our Prana or Qi to flow in a more even way.

Complete realignment is likely to require a total commitment to healing and a change to a lifestyle devoid of stress and compatible with absolute focus on the goal at hand; in other words, right action. If the patient achieves supreme balance, cure and spontaneous remission are more likely.

Brendan O'Regan and Caryle Hirshberg, in their book, *Spontaneous Remission: An Annotated Bibliography,*[3] review some of the qualities inherent in those undergoing spontaneous cure. Even if these capabilities do not come automatically, they can be nurtured as part of a self-healing practice. Each of these qualities have attributes that can be found on the right side of the Tree of Health; these attributes are noted in parentheses.

1. Having trust and regarding the disease as a challenge that can be beaten. (*Trust*)

2. Accepting the diagnosis (the truth), taking control of the situation, and having a strong fighting spirit. Assuming responsibility for the illness and one's quality of life. (*Truth, Courage*)

3. Letting go of fear and worry and not perceiving the disease as a death sentence. Embracing an attitude of being able to influence the outcome. (*Courage, Surrender*)

4. Having close relationships and a support system and being able to actively involve others with the challenge. (David Spiegel, a psychiatrist at Stanford Medical Center, showed that advanced breast cancer patients with a support group lived twice as long as those without one.)[4] (*Hope, Love*)

5. Perceiving the physician as a partner in the undertaking and being neither defiant nor passive to him or her. (*Receptivity, Knowledge*)

6. Having a strong desire to live. Wanting to complete unfulfilled goals and aspirations. (*Hope, Belief*)

7. Finding new meaning in the predicament and making major lifestyle changes. Maintaining physical fitness. (*Faith, Action*)

8. Cultivating the ability to say no. Being able to withdraw from or avoid stress and openly communicate needs. (*Courage, Choice*)

9. Having a passionate religious faith and surrendering to the will of God. (*Faith*)

They noted that those who had successfully overcome a prior life-threatening illness or serious event tended to be more successful with the present one. (This fact may validate the importance of having prevailed in a prior right of passage or trial of initiation; for example, the hero's journey.)

Ultimately, however, spontaneous remission is more an indication of grace than anything we are able to explain. We are a long way from understanding the mechanism, although vibrational alignment may be the key.

BALANCING THE SCALES

Balancing the scales implies equilibrium between the patient and the disease and can be compared to the host-parasite relationship. If the parasite kills the host, it also kills itself. A live host is necessary for the parasite's survival. If a balanced relationship occurs in which neither host nor parasite prevails, it is possible for the disease to remain stable or in remission for long periods.

However, vibrational alignment is incomplete, as is the remission. Stress of any form can upset the balance. Hard work and worry may be the biggest culprit.

The example of tuberculosis highlights the importance of balance. As medical students, we were taught that the manifestations of tuberculosis were so multiple that it could be present in almost any possible form in every organ of the body. The virulence of tuberculosis depended on homeostasis between the host and the tubercle bacteria. If the immune system was competent, the host prevailed, and this was the case in many instances where one would see a so-called Ghon focus in the lung on the chest x-ray. This told the physician that the patient had in fact been exposed to tuberculosis, but had healed the lesion without complication; however, if the patient's immune system was compromised, the body could be overcome by a deadly form of "miliary" tuberculosis. These were the two extremes of the disease spectrum, and in between were multiple manifestations of different problems affecting various organ systems. Any stress, be it traumatic, nutritional, emotional, or spiritual that would adversely affect the immune system could lead to the symptomatic manifestation of tuberculosis, even when the disease was previously only dormant.

The same principle can apply to any disease. We need to be diligent in balancing the scales between the patient or host's immune system and the disease. When this is done, many patients live for long periods in spite of their disease.

Certain patients seem to defy all odds and prognostic guesses. One of my patients, an extremely pleasant Danish man, exemplifies the principle of equanimity. He had the most aggressive form of prostate cancer and, by all standards, should have died years before he eventually passed on. The knowledge of his diagnosis seemed to have as much impact on his psyche as being told that he had just received a parking ticket. He was in harmony with himself in spite of the cancer. Although intelligent and knowledgeable about his problem, he was detached from it emotionally and seemed to feel there were more important things to life.

This detachment was not denial, but a form of surrender. There was a special quality to his psyche that allowed his immune system to be as competent as possible without any of the negative effects of morbid anxiety. In this way, it almost seemed that he had struck up a friendly relationship with his cancer, freeing his immune system to do its job effectively. He eventually died, I believe, because of a later stress related to financial burdens. He had to sell his house and move to northern California. He had no medical insurance, and for this reason he rarely came for medical care. When he would present himself at infrequent intervals, I was always amazed that he was still alive and doing well. His long remission certainly was not a result of diligent medical attention.

Such patients are rare, but they seem able to halt the progression of their disease. Their defense mechanisms are not debilitated by the prospect of death and continue to function optimally. Unfortunately, few of us have the ability to maintain this detached awareness of disease coupled with a belief that our Inner Healer can manage, even if it cannot prevail.

All healers are aware of so-called "exceptional" patients who may rigorously follow the best allopathic and nonallopathic techniques but do no better than those who don't. There are loving, cheerful, and humorous patients who die, and morose, angry, and depressed patients who survive. Ultimately, the mystery of healing remains, and no one knows all the enigmatic forces that facilitate or inhibit the Inner Healer or why certain diseases are relentless and others not. Understanding a few clues does not represent the entire picture.

Two patients stand out in my mind, both of whom had incurable prostate cancer. They were both extremely intelligent, cheerful, and positive, and availed themselves of a holistic integrated approach. In spite of their exemplary approach to the cancer, they both eventually succumbed and lived no longer than anyone else with the same stage and grade might have lived. Nevertheless, they both achieved a spirit of healing that was admirable.

However much we try to understand disease and healing, it would be arrogant to believe that we know the answer. Illness and disease are much like life itself, the great conundrum to which we have only a few answers. This saying by an anonymous writer seems to sum up all our health perplexities:

Anyone who isn't confused here, really does not understand what is going on!

RELAPSE

The disease is slowly gaining the upper hand or recurs after being in remission. The host may be in emotional turmoil because they cannot disengage from the morbid fear of the disease. Alternatively, life's tribulations, or ignorance, may prevent the patient from making the essential adjustments required to balance the energy body. Resignation may creep in at a subconscious or a conscious level. Lack of time for inner work, fear, and hopelessness result in an unhealthy "vibration," which immobilizes the Inner Healer and the immune system. Will, hope, and faith are indeterminate or nebulous, grace does not occur, and there is only a feeble effort to attain vibrational equilibrium.

FULMINATING PROGRESSION AND DEATH

This often happens to patients who seem to be doing quite well until they undergo exploratory surgery, and are "opened and closed." The surgeon abandons hope when faced with a cancer that has spread throughout the abdomen. This devastating prognostic statement to the patient may be as sinister as the worst curse given by a voodoo priest. The rapid deterioration is frequently blamed on the surgical event, but this is far less important than the psychic catastrophe that has been dealt the Inner Healer at the level of hope, faith, and will. Any attempts to regain balance seem futile. Any circumstance that can adversely impact the body's defense mechanisms can do the same thing; for example, the loss of a spouse.

Alternatively, the patient, like the imprisoned San, may welcome death as a convenient escape from life's hardships. Will is nonexistent or even negative, so belief and hope are never invoked. There is no attempt to maintain balance, and grace can manifest as a brief remission which confounds everyone; for example, someone about to die hangs on and actually looks well for another two months during the visit of a loved one. The will to live, grace, and balance occur, but are fleeting and are solely supported by an intense love connection. Demise occurs when the joy dissipates after their departure. Alternatively, grace may occur as a peaceful passing-on. Grace does not always have to mean healing and life—death may be a positive event.

BEING HEALED BUT NOT CURED

A state of inner peace is not reliant on a healthy body. Depending on our skill with transpersonal development, we can attain blissful states of being and be plagued with disease at the same time. Once we go beyond the persona or ego, profoundly altered states of consciousness avail themselves to us.

It is hard to believe that there are illuminated masters who live in the inner sanctums of their being and have no need for a healthy body. Spirit triumphs over matter, and they are beyond the physical and space and time. While difficult for ordinary mortals to comprehend, true inner health can transcend the body. Patients with incurable cancer, AIDS, and other diseases can experience a special state of equanimity. These unique individuals make terms with the Angel of Death and may have more inner peace than those around them who are in perfect physical condition.

Few escape sickness and no one escapes aging and death, which are part of the puzzle of life. As the bumper sticker proclaims, "Shit happens," and it does sometimes, in the form of incurable disease. Patients do not need to blame themselves for creating their illness, but can use illness as a way of going to the root cause of their imbalance. Correcting the cause of their inner disturbance will lead to healing and wholeness regardless of whether the disease remains or not.

This idea of maintaining equanimity conforms to the San's approach to disease—we all have sickness residing within us, and in some, illness will prevail. The San may look to the ancestral spirits as the cause of the problem, whereas we may point to the immune system. The San are much more constant in keeping their energy bodies sound and maintaining harmony.

Even with belief, hope, will, intention, and correct action, we may fail to eradicate the disease but nevertheless achieve balance, equilibrium, equanimity, and even receive grace. Joy and an incurable illness are not mutually exclusive. We do not need to be cured to be healed, and the Tree of Life can teach us this. The healing potential of the Tree of Life is portrayed by this saying of Maimonides—scholar, mystic, and court physician to Saladin several centuries ago:

> *It is a Tree of Life to those who hold it fast and all who cling to it find happiness. Its ways are ways of pleasantness and all its paths are peace.*

NOTES

1. Narby, Jeremy. *The Cosmic Serpent.* Jeremy P. Tarcher, Putnam, New York: 1998.

2. Talbot, Michael. *The Holographic Universe.* New York: Harper Perennial, New York, 1992.

3. O'Regan, Brendan and Caryle Hirshberg. *Spontaneous Remission: An Annotated Bibliography.* Sausalito: Institute of Noetic Sciences, 1993.

4. Spiegal, David, et al. *Effect of Psychological Treatment on Survival of Patients with Breast Cancer.* Lancet 1: Oct 14, 1989: 888–891.

THE SPIRIT OF HEALING

The key to inner healing is acknowledgment of our innermost feelings and fears. We will only be able to overcome them once we truly know them and, for this, we have to open our hearts.

Physicians are well aware of the fact that as medical science advances, principles they hold dear gradually erode. What was anathema yesterday is common practice today. Old habits die hard, especially when ideas that do not come from the medical journals infiltrate into the profession. Doctors have been dragged kicking and screaming into the new age of healing. Their left brain approach has served them well, but it is insufficient and they have been forced to pay attention to more right-brained, nonallopathic healing methods.

A quote from Michael de Montaigne (1533-1592) seems to sum up this age old history of inflexibilty:[1]

> *Whenever a new discovery is reported to the scientific world they say at first, It is probably not true.*
>
> *Thereafter when the truth of the proposition has been demonstrated beyond question they say, Yes, it may be true, but it is not important.*

155

Finally when sufficient time has elapsed to fully evidence its importance, they say, Yes, surely it is important but it is no longer new.

The mysticism of yesterday has indeed become the science of today, and the medical profession, at last, is beginning to realize it.

Certain psychic and shamanic healers are confident that depending on which chakra is out-of-balance, disease will eventually manifest in the organs related to that chakra. For instance, the second chakra represents the organs of reproduction and elimination, and if there is a disturbance in this chakra, these target organs are likely to be affected before any other. Shamans who make diagnoses at the level of the energy body would agree with this premise. There is no proof for this assumption but there is some anecdotal evidence for it. These healers attempt to heal the disease at the root cause. By going inward and using an altered state of consciousness, the healer can see the chakra's lack of equilibrium in the etheric body of the patient and deal with it at that level.

Western physicians frequently treat the effect of the root cause rather than the cause itself. Their approach is superficial, but successful in treating the manifestations of the disease. The intellectual exercise of diagnosis and therapy, together with high technology, makes Western medicine an alluring undertaking. Physicians are easily seduced into believing they are doing their job well, when in fact they have not gotten to the heart of the matter.

One particular patient of mine illustrated this problem. She was a young female afflicted with the perplexing problem of recurrent urinary retention (inability to void and empty the bladder), who had made repeated visits to the emergency room. I was called as the consultant urologist to evaluate the problem.

After ruling out all possible abnormalities, I noted that nothing was apparently wrong. There was no obstruction or neurological disease; the patient did not have diabetes and was not taking any drugs that might have suppressed bladder function. She fell into the category of so-called psychogenic urinary retention, thought to be an hysterical type of event in response to severe stress. The therapeutic approach was simply to allow the bladder to rest from its period of overdistention by maintaining catheter drainage for several days. Medications were given to assist the bladder to empty and to help relax the sphincter muscle so the patient could void effectively. It worked until the event recurred.

She did not admit to any current stresses or difficulties in her life, but I later learned from her psychiatrist that sexual abuse was a significant factor in her past history. The urinary system and genital system are closely connected anatomically, physiologically, and emotionally. It is not difficult to understand how the trauma of sexual abuse and the ensuing psychopathology could result in recurrent episodes of urinary retention.

As Western physicians, we are trained to fix the problem at a mechanical level; often we fail to appreciate that something is happening on a deeper plane. Even if we do appreciate it, we do not have the time to delve into it more thoroughly and exorcise the cause, as a shaman might. In this case, psychotherapy and her knowing the truth of the diagnosis was effective therapy and these episodes stopped.

When I was a medical student in Johannesburg, I was attending a busy obstetrics and gynecology clinic when a black female patient came in with a host of confusing and vague complaints. After listening for a few minutes, the gynecologist said to her, "You want babies, don't you?" She nodded her head in agreement. This was a simple example of an intuitive physician extracting an infertility problem in spite of a confusing history. The unfortunate patient was so ashamed of her plight that it was difficult for her to come straight out with her real complaint. In this era of cost containment in medicine, this type of diagnostic skill can prevent expensive and unnecessary evaluations and, at the same time, benefit the patient at a deeper level.

Often the mechanisms of disease are subtle and, since most physicians do not have the shaman's ability to diagnose clairvoyantly, the inner reason for the malady goes unattended. If doctors are to be more successful in treating their patients, they should not discount intuitive information in favor of hard objective facts, but use both to good effect. They should be both shaman and allopathic physician at the same time, and when they find their shamanic ability wanting, they should enlist the help of someone else. In the West, this shamanlike person has been called a "medical intuitive."

"Health" is a complex word, and if we are to look at all its ramifications, we have to embrace the spiritual as well as the physical. Anyone obsessed with the body only is missing the bigger picture of health. With media madness, movies, and TV hype, the body may be projected as a pure extension of ego, and taking care of it may have little more relevance to one's inner being than maintaining a new automobile—ultimately, entropy will set in and it will deteriorate. Spirit, however, can soar while the body degenerates, leading to a different level of "health."

If we are to define health better, we must look to the factors operating in a healthy body, mind, and spirit, and see what we can do to assist them.

We cannot choose our genetic makeup, but if we are disadvantaged in this area, we may have to make up for our physical deficiencies by working harder.

When it comes to unfortunate conditioning inherited as a result of unskillful parenting, we should try and understand that our parents may have done the best they could considering their circumstances. It is more constructive to forgive and try to forget than to assign blame.

The key to inner healing is acknowledgment of our innermost feelings and fears. We will only be able to overcome them once we truly know them and, for this, we have to open our hearts. We can only become intimate with ourselves and others if we become vulnerable. Vulnerability is a sign of courage and strength, not of weakness. When we become vulnerable, we can ask for help and let go of control. Forgiveness is crucial, and through it we can uncover an even greater potential to love. Unfortunately, it is much easier to erect a shield around us to protect us from hurt.

Peace of mind can be improved with physical activity and even sex. This may be a temporary way of relieving stress, and will not necessarily lead to health transformation unless done with conscious awareness and an inner-directed motivation. Moving meditations such as yoga and tai chi that direct us inward are more powerful for healing than regular exercise. Alignment of the energy flow can start with the body. A body that feels happy creates a tranquil inner being as well. Exercise, especially when internally directed, helps us move energy up the energy hierarchy. This is the reason hatha yoga has become so popular in the West. Although the postures, or *asanas*, are only a small part of yoga philosophy—the healing consequences of this form of stretching and breathing can have a miraculous effect, not only on the body but on the psyche as well.

For simplification, we could classify therapeutic techniques into outer and inner, recognizing that we are again creating duality where none should exist. The outer includes the more left-brained, cognitive, intellectual tools of allopathic medicine and science that are properties of the right side of the Tree Of Life and the sun nadi. These techniques address the body directly. The inner embrace the more mystical, receptive aspects of intuition, love, empathy, and nonallopathic healing techniques. These methods are part of the left branch of the Tree of Life and the moon channel and these connect us with the guiding capacity of the Field. We need both inner- and outer-directed techniques.

Inner techniques include:

- Relaxation, reflection, contemplation, meditation, prayer
- Writing, poetry, art
- Imagery, visualization
- Music, chanting, singing, dance, mime
- Tai chi, yoga, breath work, body movement practices
- Acupuncture and related disciplines
- Body work, massage, rolfing

- Solitude

- Ceremony, rituals, prayer, fasting

- Nature, wilderness

- Dream work

- Laughter, sex, love, or anything that promotes joy

If we have a turbulent and troubled mind, we can invoke the help of mindfulness, meditation, and other inner practices. Hypnosis, trance states, ritual, meditation, prayer, Zen, and Buddhist training have all been shown to be effective therapeutic tools.[2]

We are all given an Inner Healer and some of us are also given the gift to heal others. However, it may be difficult for us to facilitate our own Inner Healer. The proficient shaman may be able to heal others, but he cannot help himself when the die is cast. He must turn to another healer and hope for the best. We all need an adept healer in order to trigger our own Inner Healer; few of us can do it alone. When we choose, we should be sure the practitioner strengthens rather than demeans us with the capacity of their ego; they should not overpower us with their shadow side.

We must be aware of the nuances and subtleties of our own religion, culture, education, and conditioning so we can match ourselves to the right healer who can promote healing at all levels. There should be a compatibility between their awareness and consciousness and ours, which will translate into a beneficial affiliation at all levels. At the very least, there should be a willingness on behalf of the doctor to support the patient in therapies the physician may not necessarily accept.

Since few healers can cater to all these possibilities, it may be necessary to seek out more than one healer so the problem can be handled at multiple levels—surgical, medical, mental, and spiritual.

There is also healing power outside of ourselves and we should not discount the power and magic of God, grace, faith, and hope. God can enter as a form of grace at Daat on the Tree of Life at any time and prayer may promote this appearance.

Sometimes the Field exerts unusual effects on the power and energy of place; for instance, the miracles that have occurred at Lourdes. There are other "power" places that are known for their healing energy, and for me a remote cave in the Kalahari desert is one of them. Nature can be our greatest support since it incorporates all polarities and is a multifaceted reservoir for the deepest healing and the most profound personal transformation. Connecting with the earth mother and the feminine through nature is a powerful alternative healing method for communicating with knowable and unknowable aspects of the Field. Intimate contact with nature can be a receptive technique for achieving balance. There are numerous examples of patients with terminal diseases who went into remission after returning to Mother Nature for their healing and sustenance. The inner peace described in the patient with prostate cancer is easily attainable in a natural environment.

We must become ever more vigilant in protecting our outer surroundings; we cannot isolate our own well-being from the health of the place in which we live. The Aborigines believe that everything that happens in the natural world affects the dream-time. If a tree or an animal is harmed or dies, they feel it, and this manifests in their dreams. It seems that nature expresses itself to them in their dreams. The dream-time is one way they connect to and monitor nature's Field. The devastation of the natural world has become the Aboriginal nightmare, and this calamity has direct health consequences for us as well.

We can see that true health is a serious undertaking and, because of our modern lifestyle, requires significant maintenance. If we all lived happily in community and in a relationship, enjoyed a pollution-free environment, had stimulating and creative work, and plenty of free time for leisure and to attend to our bodies, there would be less need for all the stress-busting techniques available today; we could eat and drink in a more carefree way and exercise less. The toxins and time restraints of modern-day living, however, demand that we pay attention to what will give each person's particular situation the best results. Diet, exercise, and an inner practice of one form or another are crucial for all but the minority of people with superlative genetics and fortunate upbringing.

As we align ourselves more with the Field, anything becomes imaginable. We think an idea, call it something, and it becomes reality. The Internet has changed the nature of communication as we knew it; however, even the Internet is like the termite colony, an example of a knowable minifield within a Field of much greater potential. The ultimate healing occurs when we connect with our soul, our Self, or that aspect of the Divine within. Catalyzing this access will prevent us from being seduced by the allure of the commodity market and the dark side of technology.

Realizing Self is not a manifestation of selfishness and self-absorption, but rather the key to healing ourselves. When we recognize Self we also understand our interdependency and appreciate that we cannot isolate our own well-being from the wholeness of everything around us.

King Solomon told us that there is nothing new under the sun and for this reason we do not have to reinvent a new complicated approach to health. Each person can find their own specific way of creating balance and inducing the Inner Healer to heal. These words of Solomon reinforce the core belief of balance so crucial to healing, and remind us that when we are ill and it is time to heal, sometimes drastic changes are required to maintain our focus.

To every thing there is a season, and a time to every purpose under the heaven:

A time to be born and a time to die...
A time to kill and a time to heal;
A time to break down and a time to build up;
A time to weep and a time to laugh;
A time to mourn and a time to dance...
A time to get and a time to lose;
A time to keep and a time to cast away...
A time to be silent and a time to speak;
A time to love and a time to hate;
A time of war and a time of peace.

—Ecclesiastes[3]

NOTES

1. Brewerton D. *All About Arthritis.* Cambridge, Massachusetts: Harvard University Press, p. 5 (Michael de Montaigne 1533-1592), 1995.

2. O'Regan, Brendan, and Caryle Hirshberg. *Spontaneous Remission: An Annotated Bibliography.* Sausalito: Institute of Noetic Sciences, 1993.

3. *Holy Bible.* Red Letter Edition, King James Version. Iowa Falls, Iowa: World Bible Publishers.

BIBLIOGRAPHY

Brennan, Barbara Ann. *Hands of Light*. (Summary of work by Valery Hunt, UCLA 1977, and Dr. Hiroshi Montoyama, Tokyo, Japan I.A.R.P., 1979.) New York: Bantam Books, 1987.

Brewerton D. *All About Arthritis*. Cambridge, Massachusetts: Harvard University Press, p. 5 (Michael de Montaigne 1533-1592), 1995.

Calderon, Eduardo, Richard Cowan, Douglas Sharon, and F. Kaye Sharon. *Eduardo el Curandero: The Words of a Peruvian Healer*. Richmond, Louisiana: North Atlantic Books, 1987.

Chopra, Deepak, M.D. *Perfect Health*. New York: Harmony Books, 1991.

———. *Quantum Healing, Exploring the Frontiers of Mind Body Medicine*. New York: Bantam, 1990.

Cousins, Norman. *Anatomy of an Illness*. New York: Norton, 1995.

Cumes, David. *Inner Passages, Outer Journeys*. St. Paul, Minnesota: Llewellyn Publications, 1998.

Devereux, Paul. *Shamanism and the Mystery Lines*. St. Paul, Minnesota: Llewellyn Publications, 1993.

Dossey, Larry, M.D. *Healing Words*. San Francisco: Harper Collins, 1994.

Dowson, Thomas A. *Rock Engravings of Southern Africa*. Johannesburg: Witwatersrand University Press, 1992.

Epstein, Pearl. *Kabbalah: The Way of the Jewish Mystic*. Boston, MA: Shambhala, 1972.

Feuerstein, Georg. *The Encyclopedic Dictionary of Yoga*. New York: Paragon House, 1990.

———. *Yoga: The Technology of Ecstasy*. Los Angeles: Jeremy P. Tarcher, Inc., 1989.

Garfield, Charles. *Peak Performance: Mental Training Techniques of the World's Greatest Athletes*. New York: Warner Books, 1984.

Gerber, Richard, M.D. *Vibrational Medicine*. Chapter 4 summary of work by Montoyama and Bentov. Santa Fe, New Mexico: Bear & Co., 1988.

Graham, Rae. *Tales of the African Life*. Capetown: Struck Books, 1992.

Hadingham, Evan. *Lines to the Mountain Gods*. New York: Random House, 1987.

Halifax, Joah, Ph.D. *Shamanic Voices*. New York: E.P. Dutton, 1979.

Hammond-Tooke, David. *Rituals and Medicines*. Capetown, South Africa: Creda Press, 1989.

Holy Bible. Red Letter Edition, King James Version. Iowa Falls, Iowa: World Bible Publishers.

Hunt, Valery, et al. "Abstract. A Study of Structural Integration from Neuromuscular, Energy Field and Emotional Approaches." Sponsored by the Rolf Institute of Structural Integration, 1977.

Johari, Harish. *Chakras Energy Centers of Transformation*. Vermont: Destiny Books, 1987.

Kaplan, Rachel, and Stephen Kaplan. *The Experience of Nature*. New York: Cambridge University Press, 1989.

Katz, Richard. *Boiling Energy*. Cambridge, Massachusetts: Harvard University Press, 1982.

Katz, Richard, Megan Biesele, and Verna St. John. *Healing Makes Our Hearts Happy*. Rochester, Vermont: Inner Traditions, 1996.

Lamb, Bruce. *Wizard of the Upper Amazon.* Boston: Houghton Mifflin Company, 1974.

Lewis-Williams, J. D., and T. A. Dowson. "The Signs of All Times, Entoptic Phenomena in Upper Paleolithic Art," *Current Anthropology*, vol. 29, no. 2, April 1988.

———. *Images of Power: Understanding Bushman Rock Art.* Johannesburg: Southern Book Publishers, 1989.

Madhi, Louise Carus, Steven Foster, and Meredith Little. *Betwixt and Between: Patterns of Masculine and Feminine Initiation.* La Salle, Illinois: Open Court, 1988.

Maslow, A. H. *The Farther Reaches of Human Nature.* New York: Penguin, 1976.

Mckenna, Terence. *Food of the Gods.* New York: Bantam Books, 1992.

Mookerjee, Ajit. *Kundalini: The Arousal of Inner Energy.* London: Thames and Hudson, 1989.

Muktanada, Swami. *The Play of Consciousness.* San Francisco: Harper & Row, 1978.

Narby, Jeremy and Jeremy P. Tarcher. *The Cosmic Serpent.* New York: Putnam, 1998.

O'Regan, Brendan and Caryle Hirshberg. *Spontaneous Remission: An Annotated Bibliography.* Sausalito: Institute of Noetic Sciences, 1993.

Ornish, Dean. *Love and Survival.* New York: Harper Collins, 1998.

Pentateuch and Haftorahs, from Genesis, edited by Dr. J. H. Hertz. London: Soncino Press, 1981.

"Positive Therapeutic Effects of Intercessory Prayer in a Coronary Care Unit Population," *Southern Medical Journal*, vol. 81, no. 7. July 1988, 826-829.

Radin, Dean. "Moving Mind. Moving Matter." (extract from *The Conscious Universe*) *Noetic Sciences Review*, no. 46. Summer 1998.

Ring, Kenneth. *Life at Death*. New York: Quill, 1980.

Shimon Halevi, Zev ben. *Kabbalah Tradition of Hidden Knowledge*. London: Thames and Hudson, 1992.

Siegel, Bernie. *Love, Medicine and Miracles: Lessons Learned from a Surgeon's Experience with Exceptional Patients*. New York: Harper Row, 1990.

Some, Malidoma Patrice. *The Healing Wisdom of Africa*. New York: Penguin Putnam, Inc., 1998.

Spiegal, David, et al. *Effect of Psychological Treatment on Survival of Patients with Breast Cancer*. Lancet 1: October 14, 1989: 888–891.

Talbot, Michael. *The Holographic Universe*. New York: Harper Perennial, 1991.

The Bhagavad-Gita, translated by Swami Prabhavananda and Christopher Isherwood. England: Phoenix House, 1972.

Van der Post, Laurens and Jane Taylor. *Testament to the Bushmen*. London: Penguin, Rainbird Publishing Group, 1984.

Van Gennup, Arnold. *The Rites of Passage*. Chicago: The University of Chicago Press, 1996.

Wolf, Fred Alan. *The Eagles Quest*. New York: Summit Books, 1991.

Targ, Elisabeth. "Distant Healing." *Noetic Sciences Review,* no. 49. August–November 1999: 24.

INDEX

☾ REACH FOR THE MOON

Llewellyn publishes hundreds of books on your favorite subjects! To get these exciting books, including the ones on the following pages, check your local bookstore or order them directly from Llewellyn.

ORDER BY PHONE

- Call toll-free within the U.S. and Canada, 1-800-THE MOON
- In Minnesota, call (651) 291-1970
- We accept VISA, MasterCard, and American Express

ORDER BY MAIL

- Send the full price of your order (MN residents add 7% sales tax) in U.S. funds, plus postage & handling to:

  Llewellyn Worldwide
  P.O. Box 64383, Dept. K196-1
  St. Paul, MN 55164–0383, U.S.A.

POSTAGE & HANDLING
(For the U.S., Canada, and Mexico)

- $4.00 for orders $15.00 and under
- $5.00 for orders over $15.00
- No charge for orders over $100.00

We ship UPS in the continental United States. We ship standard mail to P.O. boxes. Orders shipped to Alaska, Hawaii, The Virgin Islands, and Puerto Rico are sent first-class mail. Orders shipped to Canada and Mexico are sent surface mail.

International orders: Airmail—add freight equal to price of each book to the total price of order, plus $5.00 for each non-book item (audio tapes, etc.).

Surface mail—Add $1.00 per item.

Allow 2 weeks for delivery on all orders.
Postage and handling rates subject to change.

DISCOUNTS

We offer a 20% discount to group leaders or agents. You must order a minimum of 5 copies of the same book to get our special quantity price.

FREE CATALOG

Get a free copy of our color catalog, New Worlds of Mind and Spirit. Subscribe for just $10.00 in the United States and Canada ($30.00 overseas, airmail). Many bookstores carry New Worlds—ask for it!

Visit our website at www.llewellyn.com for more information.

Inner Passages, Outer Journeys
*Wilderness, Healing, and the
Discovery of Self*

David Cumes, M.D.

Whether you scale the sides of mountains or just putter in the garden, wilderness healer David Cumes, M.D., shows you how nature can be one of the most powerful and accessible forms of self-healing.

Few are prepared to commit to the rigors of disciplined spiritual practice. It is through nature that we can connect with our higher self most easily. The outer wilderness helps us access the inner wilderness of our psyches. When approached with the right frame of mind, wilderness can facilitate "peak experiences."

This book is for those with an adventurous spirit who may or may not have defined their spiritual path. It addresses the psychospiritual, healing and restorative effects of nature, and describes how to amplify your experience through transformational practices. This book is the first of its kind to combine the spirituality of the last surviving hunter gatherers of Africa with the ancient wisdom of yoga, Kabbalah and shamanism.

1-56718-195-3
6 x 9, 192 pp., illus. $12.95

To order, call 1-800 THE MOON
Prices subject to change without notice

Teachings of a Grand Master
A Dialogue of Martial Arts & Spirituality

Richard Behrens

He can pin a man to the floor without touching him. He can stand on one foot and hold off twenty-two power lifters and professional football players. Considered one of the foremost martial arts masters in the world, he counsels Wall Street moguls, world-class athletes, even military hand-to-hand combat instructors.

Now Richard Behrens reveals the esoteric principles behind Torishimaru Aiki Jutsu, the only martial art in the world that allows its practitioners to control an attacker's movements and weapons without the use of physical contact. What's more, he shows how anyone can apply these same principles to everyday life events.

The book follows a question and answer format and is divided into four sections. The first focuses on the Torishimaru Aiki Jutsu and its novice techniques and principles of control. The second discusses meditation and the nature of the mind. In section three, Behrens shares thirty-three deep spiritual insights, and in section four he explains how to apply the martial arts principles to life and the world of business.

1-56718-060-4
6 x 9, 416 pp. $17.95

To order, call 1-800 THE MOON
Prices subject to change without notice

The Lost Secrets of Prayer
Practices for Self-Awakening

Guy Finley

Do your prayers go unanswered? Or when they are answered, do the results bring you only *temporary* relief or happiness? If so, you may be surprised to learn that there are actually two kinds of prayer, and the kind that most of us practice is actually the *least* effective.

Best-selling author Guy Finley presents *The Lost Secrets of Prayer,* a guide to the *second* kind of prayer. The purpose of true prayer, as revealed in the powerful insights that make up this book, is not to appeal for what you think you want. Rather, it is to bring you to the point where you are no longer blocked from seeing that everything you need is *already here*. When you begin praying in this new way, you will discover a higher awareness of your present self. Use these age-old yet forgotten practices for self-awakening and your life will never be the same.

1-56718-276-3
5¼ x 8, 240 pp. $9.95

To order, call 1-800 THE MOON
Prices subject to change without notice